"*The American war is over: but this is far from being the case with the American Revolution. On the contrary, nothing but the first act of the drama is closed.*"

—DR. BENJAMIN RUSH, SIGNER OF THE DECLARATION OF INDEPENDENCE AND
SURGEON GENERAL OF THE CONTINENTAL ARMY, JANUARY 25, 1787

The Museum's first floor rotunda includes the orientation film *Revolution* in the Lenfest Myer Theater, as well as the Cross Keys Café, museum shop, and Patriots Gallery. The 1836 *Siege of Yorktown* hangs in the Oneida Indian Nation Atrium on the second floor, drawing visitors up to the core exhibit galleries.

Museum of the American Revolution

* * * OFFICIAL GUIDEBOOK * * *

BECKON BOOKS

The Museum of the American Revolution opened to the public on April 19, 2017, the anniversary of the opening shots of the Revolution at the Battles of Lexington and Concord.

About the Museum of the American Revolution

In 1903, during a sermon commemorating George Washington's birthday, Reverend W. Herbert Burk of All Saints' Episcopal Church in Norristown, Pennsylvania, announced an ambitious plan to construct a memorial to Washington in Valley Forge. While Washington Memorial Chapel was being built, Burk also began acquiring artifacts as part of a dream to found a national museum dedicated to America's founding. In 1907, he launched a two-year fund-raising effort to acquire Washington's original Revolutionary War tent. Burk opened a small museum within the chapel in 1909. In 1918, he established the Valley Forge Historical Society.

This early 20th-century photograph shows parts of General Washington's original sleeping and office tent. Reverend Burk purchased it from Mary Custis Lee, Robert E. Lee's daughter.

In 2003, the Museum of the American Revolution was created and inherited the Valley Forge Historical Society's collection. These efforts culminated in a historic land exchange with the National Park Service in 2010, when the Museum acquired the site of the former Independence National Historical Park Visitor Center in exchange for 78 acres of privately owned land in Valley Forge. The Park Service was eager to acquire the parcel, which was adjacent to Valley Forge National Historical Park—and the Museum was thrilled to secure an ideal location in the heart of Philadelphia's historic district.

The Museum began a $150 million campaign in 2010 to endow, build, and open the Museum of the American Revolution. During the demolition and construction process, the Museum was sensitive to the site's history, initiating an archaeological excavation. Archaeologists found 85,000 artifact pieces, most of them from brick-lined privy and well shafts that were sealed beneath a later generation of buildings removed from the site.

Thanks to the generosity of H. F. "Gerry" and Marguerite Lenfest, along with 19,000 private individuals from all 50 states, the Commonwealth of Pennsylvania, the Oneida Indian Nation, and foundations and corporate support, the Museum of the American Revolution opened to the public on April 19, 2017. Today, the Museum houses a rich collection of Revolutionary-era weapons, personal items, letters, diaries, and works of art. It also includes immersive galleries, theater experiences, and re-created historical environments. These elements bring the events, people, and ideals of the nation's founding to life and engage people in the history and continuing relevance of the American Revolution.

W. Herbert Burk assembled what became the core of the Museum's collection.

BEHIND THE SCENES

The main stairwell of the Museum is dominated by the *Siege of Yorktown*. This copy of the 1836 original (by Louis Charles-Auguste Couder) was painted by Henry LeGrand and first exhibited in 1860. Three notable New York firms contributed to the painting's conservation, stretching, varnishing, and framing of the 14-by-17-foot canvas. Once conservation was complete, it took five days for the painting to be mounted in its nearly 1,000-pound frame and hung.

Unearthing History

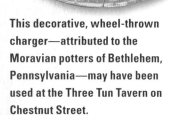

During preconstruction work, archaeologists conducted a dig at the site, searching through the soil by hand and by wire screen to discover thousands of artifacts dating from the 1600s to the 1900s. Each artifact was carefully recorded with details that included where it was located in the archaeological feature (such as a privy or well). Archaeologists also indicated the artifact's proximity to other items to provide context for its story. The result was a 480-page archaeological record of the development of Philadelphia in microcosm.

The study captured the physical changes to the site as well as the human activities that took place within it, highlighting both the artifacts and the people who threw them out. The earliest assemblage of artifacts came from a feature associated with a small house that was located on the eastern edge of the site and probably belonged to a tanner. Another assemblage dating to the 1730s appeared to have come from a tavern on Chestnut Street and included many redware ceramics made by identifiable local potters.

Among the most extraordinary artifacts came from an unlicensed tavern on Carter's Alley, where a punch bowl emblazoned with the picture of the brigantine *Triphena* was found.

Nearly 400 artifacts were found at the site of the eight-story Jayne Building, which changed Carter's Alley to a primarily commercial site by the middle of the 1800s. The arrival of the Lippincott button factory transformed the alley to an industrial site, and it then became a cultural attraction after the National Park Service constructed its visitor center there in the 1970s.

The archaeological data in the report not only provided a clearer picture of the past, it also served as a future resource for other historians, scholars, and scientists. Some of the collections from the site are curated by the Commonwealth of Pennsylvania in Harrisburg; other artifacts directly connected to the American Revolution are curated at the Museum.

This decorative, wheel-thrown charger—attributed to the Moravian potters of Bethlehem, Pennsylvania—may have been used at the Three Tun Tavern on Chestnut Street.

Artifacts were taken back to the lab, sorted by type and time period, and reassembled. Soil samples were studied for traces of plant-based foods and products to help determine the food a household may have eaten.

Working alongside construction workers, archaeologists excavated the site of the Museum in 2014 and 2015. Here they are excavating portions of Carter's Alley.

The American Revolution: 1760–1776

✴ **October 25, 1760:** King George III succeeds to the British throne.

1763: In what comes to be called Pontiac's War, western Indian nations band together to try and drive the British out of their lands in Ohio and around the Great Lakes.

February 10, 1763: The Treaty of Paris takes effect, leaving Great Britain with vast French and Spanish territories in North America.

March 22, 1765: Parliament passes the Stamp Tax to pay for the defense of the newly expanded American colonies.

1767: Parliament passes the Townshend Acts to raise revenue in the colonies and strengthen enforcement of trade regulations. These include the Suspending Act, which suspends the New York government until it will abide by the Quartering Act.

1767: John Dickinson publishes his views in *Letters from a Farmer in Pennsylvania*, urging the colonies to unite and fight to restore the rights Great Britain has taken away.

October 1768: British troops land in Boston, stirring anti-British political sentiment.

July 22, 1769: Charleston, South Carolina, adopts a "non-importation agreement," joining other American cities in boycotting British exports.

✴ **March 5, 1770:** British soldiers, feeling threatened, fire into a Boston mob. This event, which ultimately kills five, becomes known as the Boston Massacre.

December 16, 1773: A crowd dumps crates of British tea into Boston Harbor, an act known as the Boston Tea Party. In response, Parliament passes the so-called Intolerable Acts.

1774: Following the Boston Tea Party, the British enact the Intolerable Acts, also known as the Coercive Acts, to punish New England and Massachusetts in particular.

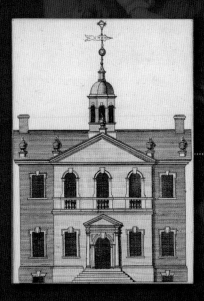

✴ **September 5, 1774:** The First Continental Congress convenes in Carpenters' Hall in Philadelphia to consider a response to the Intolerable Acts.

✳ **April 19, 1775:** The first military engagement of the American Revolution at Lexington and Concord is sparked when British forces attempt to seize military supplies from the Massachusetts militia and capture Samuel Adams and John Hancock.

May 10, 1775: The Second Continental Congress convenes in Philadelphia.

June 14, 1775: Congress votes to create the Continental Army and appoints George Washington as commander in chief.

June 17, 1775: British troops dislodge an entrenched New England force in the Battle of Bunker Hill but suffer more than 1,000 casualties.

November 7, 1775: Virginia's royal governor, John Murray, 4th Earl of Dunmore, declares martial law and promises freedom to the enslaved African Americans who join his British forces.

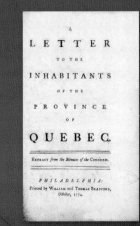

✳ **December 31, 1775:** American forces attack Quebec in a failed attempt to drive British forces from the province and enlist Canadian support for the American cause.

January 1776: Thomas Paine publishes *Common Sense*, suggesting that America should break away from Great Britain.

March 17, 1776: British General Sir William Howe evacuates Boston after American troops fortify Dorchester Heights.

June 28, 1776: British land and naval forces are repulsed at Fort Sullivan, near Charleston, South Carolina.

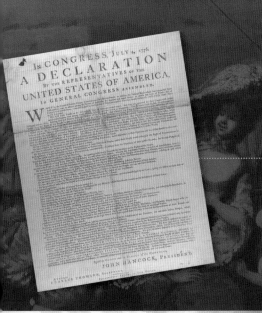

✳ **July 2, 1776:** The Second Continental Congress votes to sever political ties with Great Britain. Public announcement and publication of the Declaration of Independence occurs on July 4.

August 27, 1776: British land and naval forces attack the Continental Army on Long Island. Over the next several weeks, the British forces defeat the Americans around New York and across New Jersey.

✳ **September 15, 1776:** After weeks of fighting, New York City falls to the British. They hold the city for the rest of the war.

December 25, 1776: Washington crosses the Delaware and surprises the Hessian garrison of Trenton, New Jersey. Over the next 10 days, the struggle for American independence is revived.

The American Revolution: 1777–1790

September 11, 1777: Washington's army is driven from the field during the Battle of Brandywine, the largest land battle of the war. Howe's force occupies Philadelphia two weeks later.

✳ **October 17, 1777:** British General John Burgoyne's surrender at Saratoga influences France's decision to declare war on Great Britain.

✳ **December 19, 1777:** Washington's bedraggled forces arrive at Valley Forge, about 20 miles northwest of British-occupied Philadelphia, where they remain for six months.

February 6, 1778: The Continental Congress and the French government sign a treaty of alliance.

June 28, 1778: British and American forces clash in central New Jersey in the Battle of Monmouth.

July 4, 1778: Virginian George Rogers Clark leads an expedition of militias from Kentucky and western Virginia against the British-held village of Kaskaskia in the Illinois Country.

✳ **June 21, 1779:** Spain declares war on Great Britain, joining France in naval and land operations against the British.

June 30, 1779: British General Sir Henry Clinton issues the Philipsburg Proclamation urging enslaved African Americans in Virginia to run away and join the British Army.

August 29, 1779: Native Americans and Loyalists defend against invading American forces in the territory of the Six Nations during the Battle of Newtown.

✳ **May 12, 1780:** British General Sir Henry Clinton captures Charleston.

October 7, 1780: Backcountry militias defeat Loyalist forces at the Battle of Kings Mountain, halting the British invasion of North Carolina.

January 1, 1781: Pennsylvania troops mutiny in their camp near Morristown, New Jersey, during one of the coldest winters in the 1700s.

January 17, 1781: The dramatic American victory at the Battle of Cowpens reinvigorates southern support for the Revolution.

March 15, 1781: British forces defeat Americans under Nathanael Greene at the Battle of Guilford Courthouse.

✴ **October 19, 1781:** After weeks of fighting, British General Charles Cornwallis surrenders to a combined American and French force in Yorktown.

July 13, 1782: A force of Six Nations warriors, accompanied by Loyalist and British volunteers, destroys Hanna's Town in western Pennsylvania.

November 30, 1782: The United States and Great Britain sign preliminary articles of peace that recognize American independence and cede to the United States a vast stretch of territory.

September 3, 1783: The Treaty of Paris ends the American War of Independence and is later ratified in 1784.

November 25, 1783: British forces evacuate New York City.

December 23, 1783: General Washington resigns from the Continental Army.

✴ **August 29, 1786:** Shays' Rebellion begins in western Massachusetts. The rebels, who are Revolutionary War veterans, are angry at what they see as the new nation's oppressive political and economic policies. After the rebellion is stopped, calls for a stronger national government to prevent such uprisings grow.

May–September 1787: Delegates convene in Philadelphia to revise the Articles of Confederation. This body frames the United States Constitution.

✴ **April 30, 1789:** George Washington is sworn in as the first president of the United States of America under its new Constitution.

The Museum's realistic re-creation of the first
Liberty Tree in Boston includes a fragment from
the last standing Liberty Tree, which stood in
Annapolis, Maryland, until 1999.

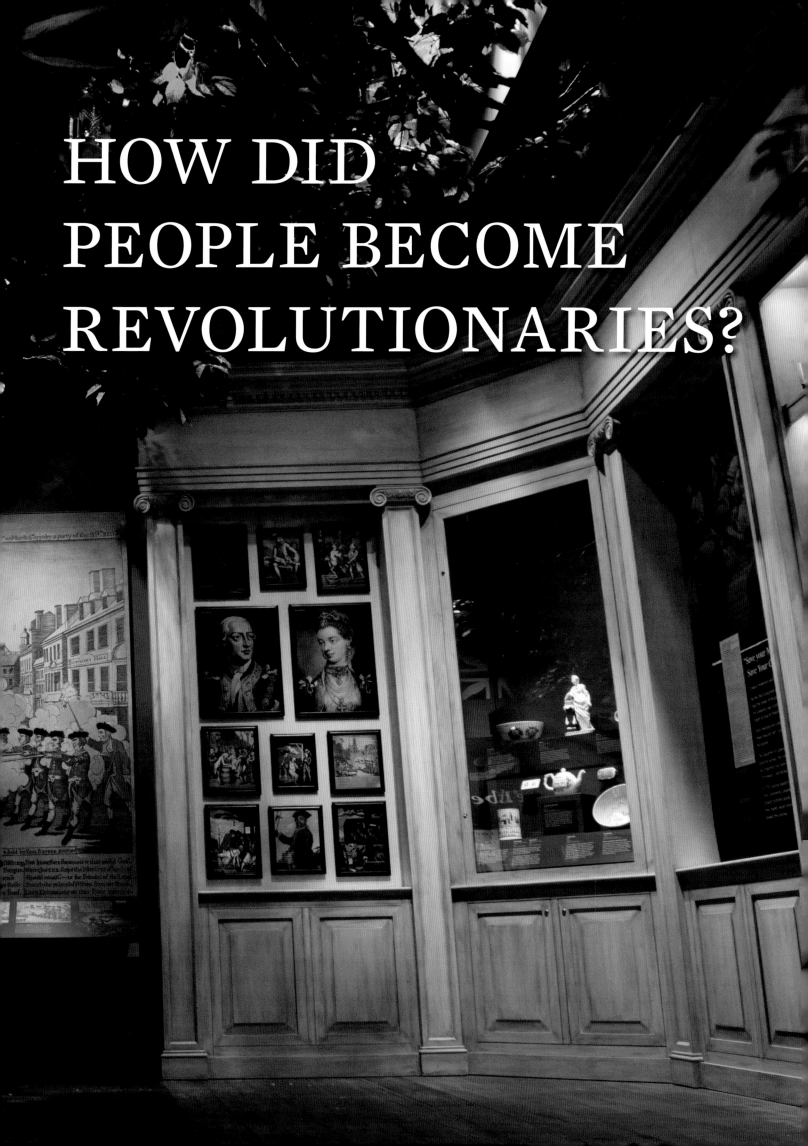

HOW DID
PEOPLE BECOME
REVOLUTIONARIES?

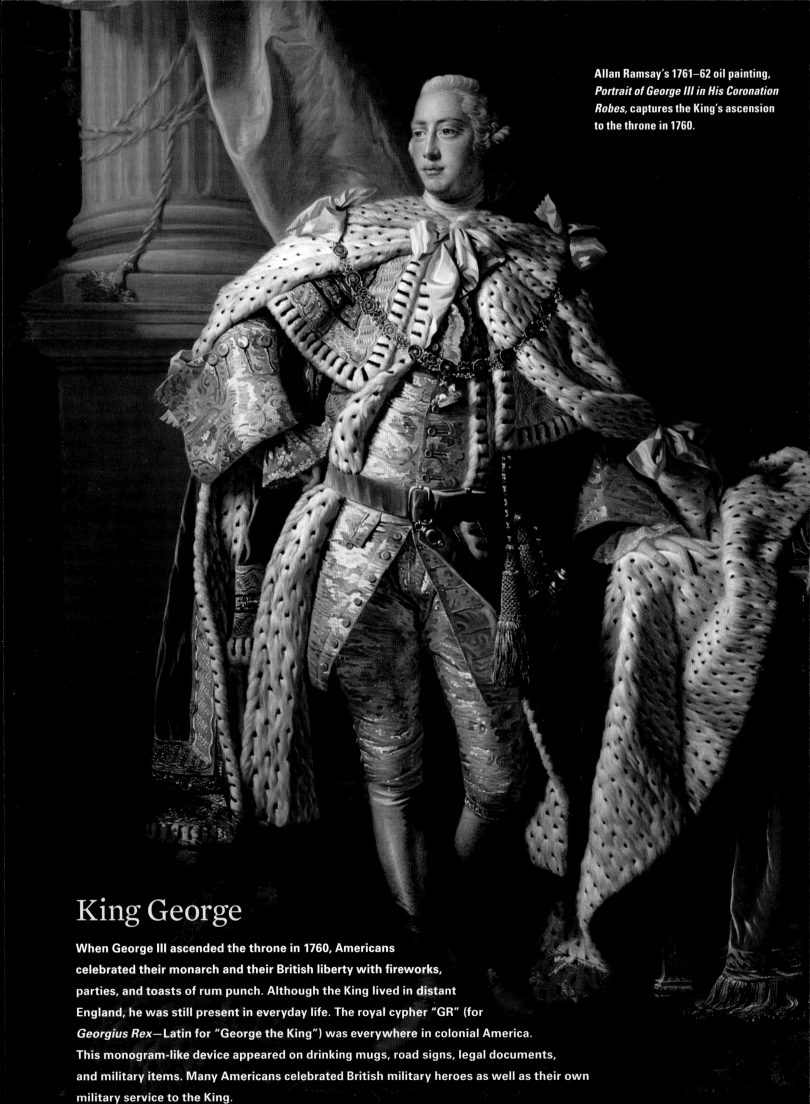

Allan Ramsay's 1761–62 oil painting, *Portrait of George III in His Coronation Robes,* captures the King's ascension to the throne in 1760.

King George

When George III ascended the throne in 1760, Americans celebrated their monarch and their British liberty with fireworks, parties, and toasts of rum punch. Although the King lived in distant England, he was still present in everyday life. The royal cypher "GR" (for *Georgius Rex*—Latin for "George the King") was everywhere in colonial America. This monogram-like device appeared on drinking mugs, road signs, legal documents, and military items. Many Americans celebrated British military heroes as well as their own military service to the King.

British America

In 1763, many British Americans were proud to be part of the most powerful empire in the history of the world. In that year, a peace treaty between Britain, France, and Spain ended the Seven Years' War. This victory gave Britain an empire that stretched around the globe, including all the lands east of the Mississippi River.

Perhaps two million or more colonists inhabited this land. Most of these colonists celebrated Britain—and King George III—as the greatest protector of liberty in the world. They believed that the King would provide them with order, peace, religious freedom, and the right to representation.

In addition to the British colonists, there were another million or more people living on these lands. They included Native Americans, former French and Spanish colonists, and enslaved and free African Americans. Their relationship to the British crown, and to their colonial neighbors, was complicated.

Native Americans had to decide to fight or to accept that the British had claimed the land that had been their home for thousands of years. Some hoped the King would help them protect their lands from colonial settlers. Others thought that war was the best strategy for safeguarding their homes.

Former Spanish and French colonists had to decide if they wanted to assimilate into British culture. However, French colonists hoped that King George III would protect their Catholic and native religious traditions.

About one in five Americans was enslaved, some born in America and others captured and carried across the Atlantic from Africa. Some enslaved African Americans whispered rumors that King George III might have sympathy for their cause.

But virtually no one expected large numbers of Britain's colonists who had fought for the empire in the last war to have a problem with their king. The next decade proved that in politics, nothing is certain.

After the Seven Years' War ended in 1763, French Canadians, like other non-British North Americans, had to live under a British king.

The Westerwald region of Germany produced stoneware ceramics, marked "GR" for King George, for both England and the American colonies.

Decade of Resistance

The Stamp Act of 1765 required most documents to be printed on taxed paper. An emblem was printed or attached to the paper to prove the tax had been paid.

Britain's 1763 victory in the Seven Years' War brought turmoil rather than peace. Britain claimed millions of acres of French, Spanish, and Indian lands in North America—but this territory saddled the empire with massive political and economic challenges.

In 1763, some Native American nations rose up against British forces and forts in their homeland, in what was called Pontiac's War. To ease tensions, King George closed Indian lands to new settlement, stationing troops in frontier forts to keep peace. Then the British Parliament imposed a tax—the Stamp Act of 1765—to support these troops.

To the British government, this tax on legal documents and other paper seemed reasonable. In England, people had been paying stamp taxes for nearly a century. The Stamp Act was expected to raise less than half of the cost of supporting the British Army in America. Americans, however, saw the Stamp Act as an invasion of their rights. They felt taxes should only be imposed through their own elected legislatures. "No taxation without representation" became their rallying cry.

Parliament repealed the Stamp Act and replaced it with another set of taxes, but Americans opposed those too. Tensions grew, particularly in Boston, where the British Army sent regiments to protect customs officials in 1768. Violence exploded when a crowd attacked a British guard on March 5, 1770, culminating in an event the colonists called the Boston Massacre.

In 1773, the British government tried to boost the struggling East India Company with an exclusive right to import tea directly to America from London. But Americans interpreted the Tea Act as creating an unfair monopoly and as clever persuasion. On the night of December 16, 1773, colonists dressed as Indians boarded a tea ship in Boston Harbor, dumping the contents into the water.

The British government responded swiftly. Parliament imposed the Coercive Acts, which included closing the port of Boston to trade, suspending the government charter of Massachusetts, and establishing military law in the colony.

People throughout the American colonies, however, sympathized with Massachusetts. Suddenly, the colonists were unified beyond anything the Americans could have accomplished on their own.

This 1789 British engraving from a children's book is one of the earliest depictions of what became known as the Boston Tea Party.

Boston silversmith and Son of Liberty Paul Revere produced this image of the Boston Massacre in 1770. His engraving distorted the scene by showing the Boston crowd as innocent and the British soldiers as deliberate murderers.

BUTCHER'S HALL

Engrav'd Printed & Sold by PAUL REVERE BOSTON

Mercy Otis Warren

Mercy Otis Warren was perhaps the leading female political writer of the colonial resistance. She was married to James Warren, a representative in the Massachusetts legislature, and hosted meetings of future Revolutionaries at her home. As a woman, she was prohibited from holding office, so she used her pen to shape public opinion. In June 1774, Warren published a poem in the *Royal American Magazine* urging each American woman to use homespun cloth and "lay her female ornaments aside." Her published poetry, plays, and private correspondence galvanized American colonial protests against British actions.

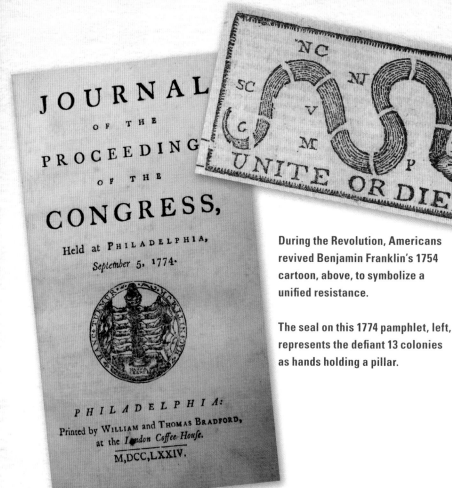

During the Revolution, Americans revived Benjamin Franklin's 1754 cartoon, above, to symbolize a unified resistance.

The seal on this 1774 pamphlet, left, represents the defiant 13 colonies as hands holding a pillar.

BEHIND THE SCENES

During their site dig, archaeologists discovered sherds of a 1760s punch bowl made in Liverpool, England. The bowl commemorates the *Triphena*, a British merchant ship that sailed out of Philadelphia in the 1760s. In 1765, the *Triphena* carried an appeal from Philadelphia merchants to merchants in Liverpool requesting their help in lobbying Parliament to repeal the Stamp Act.

> "We consider the cause of the Town of Boston as the common cause of British America and as suffering in defense of the Rights of the Colonies in general."
> —WILMINGTON, NORTH CAROLINA, CALL FOR A PROVINCIAL CONGRESS, 1774

John Wilkes

Radicals in Britain and America celebrated John Wilkes as a champion of British liberty. Wilkes, a Londoner, published a radical newspaper called the *North Briton*. His 45th issue criticized the King. Even as Wilkes faced imprisonment for this and other writings, he was elected to Parliament. When other members of Parliament refused him his seat and ordered a new election, Wilkes ran again. He won four straight times despite these charges.

For American radicals, Wilkes's cause came to symbolize the principle of freedom of the press and the dangers of a corrupt Parliament. Supporters of Wilkes displayed the number 45 on their clothing, drinking vessels, snuffboxes, and other personal items.

Printed in London, this image cast the Americans as a violent and low-status mob. It depicted Americans about to force John Malcolm, a tax official, to drink tea after being tarred and feathered on January 25, 1774.

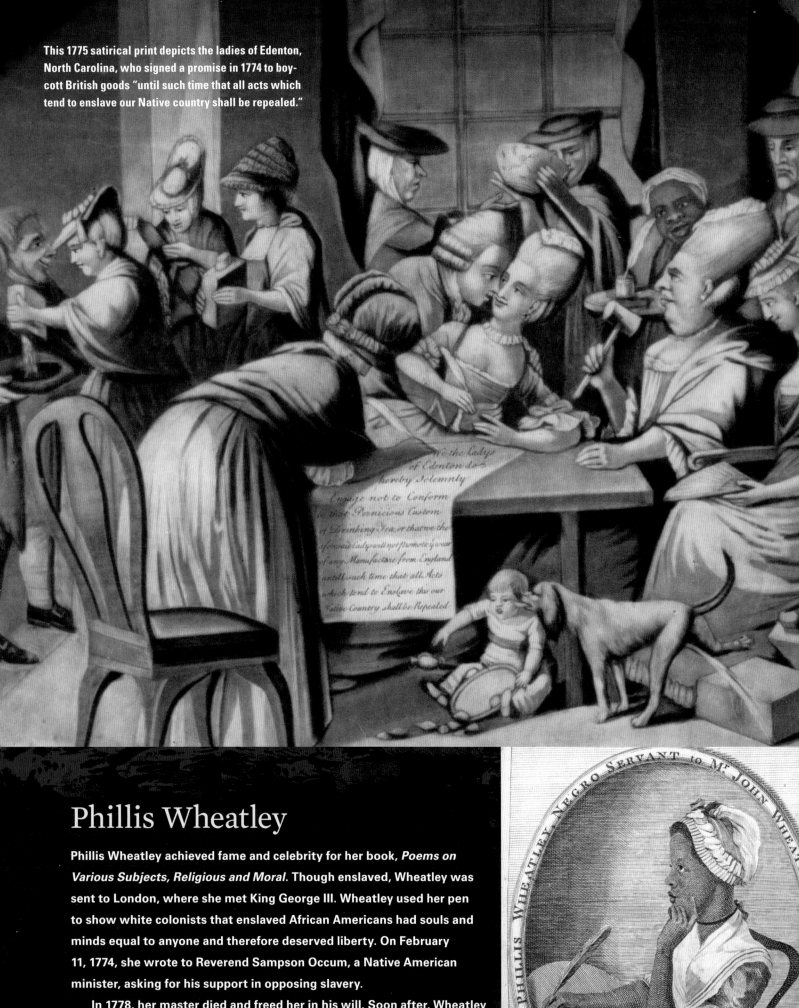

This 1775 satirical print depicts the ladies of Edenton, North Carolina, who signed a promise in 1774 to boycott British goods "until such time that all acts which tend to enslave our Native country shall be repealed."

Phillis Wheatley

Phillis Wheatley achieved fame and celebrity for her book, *Poems on Various Subjects, Religious and Moral*. Though enslaved, Wheatley was sent to London, where she met King George III. Wheatley used her pen to show white colonists that enslaved African Americans had souls and minds equal to anyone and therefore deserved liberty. On February 11, 1774, she wrote to Reverend Sampson Occum, a Native American minister, asking for his support in opposing slavery.

In 1778, her master died and freed her in his will. Soon after, Wheatley married a free African American man. When her husband was imprisoned for debt in 1784, she had to work as a domestic servant. She died on December 4, 1784.

Liberty for All?

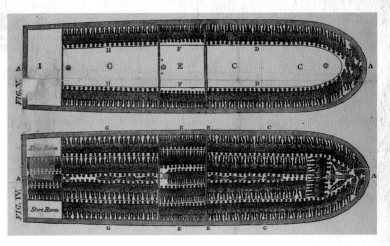

As Parliament cracked down, the colonists got organized. The Sons and Daughters of Liberty formed to channel popular outrage. The first Liberty Tree, a large elm in Boston, was a gathering place for Sons and Daughters of Liberty from 1765 to 1775. Other colonial towns adopted their own Liberty Trees, which became symbols of resistance to British tyranny.

Resistance spread through the colonies, with women urging boycotts of British goods. As the chief consumers of household goods, women held the power of the purse. The Daughters of Liberty ensured that these boycotts worked. Many of them began producing homespun alternatives to imports. As tensions grew, the colonists became more bold and violent in their protests. Some Americans even hung life-like effigies of British officials in public to be mocked or burned.

The colonists also organized a more official means of coordinating their resistance. Comprised of representatives from 12 colonies, the First Continental Congress met in Carpenters' Hall in Philadelphia in 1774. It called for new governments where royal governors had dissolved elected colonial legislatures, organized an association for boycotting, and endorsed preparations for war.

Even before white colonists battled for political liberty, African Americans sought personal freedom. As resistance to British political "slavery" grew, some colonial leaders—including James Otis of Massachusetts, Benjamin Rush of Philadelphia, and Richard Henry Lee of Virginia—argued that American slavery and American freedom were incompatible. Word also spread through enslaved communities that an English court case, the Somerset Decision of 1772, had declared slavery inconsistent with English liberty.

In 1773, a group of enslaved African Americans petitioned the Royal Military Governor Thomas Gage to pass a law for the right to buy their freedom. "We expect great things," the petitioners wrote, "from men who have made such a noble stand against the designs of their fellow-men to enslave them." In 1774, another group of enslaved people also petitioned Governor Gage to pass a law emancipating them.

When war broke out in 1775, enslaved people had to decide who offered the more likely route to freedom: the British or the Americans? Thousands of African Americans joined the Continental Army. But for many enslaved people, freedom wore a red coat. Tens of thousands fled their American masters for British camps.

This widely publicized drawing of a slave ship, published by an abolitionist in 1787, showed the inhumane conditions for newly enslaved people during their transportation from Africa to the colonies.

"... that we may obtain our Natural right, our freedoms, and out [sic] children be set liberty."
—*Petition of a Grate Number of Blackes*, WRITTEN TO THOMAS GAGE, BRITISH GOVERNOR OF MASSACHUSETTS, 1774

The Shot Heard Round the World

Did You Know?

Despite what many have heard, Paul Revere was just one of more than a dozen alarm riders on April 18 and 19, 1775.

The Revolutionary War began on April 19, 1775, in the towns of Lexington and Concord, Massachusetts. It had been a decade since the Stamp Act first sparked American resistance to British authority.

On April 18, British General Thomas Gage dispatched 700 soldiers from Boston to capture resistance leaders John Hancock and Samuel Adams in Lexington and to destroy military supplies at Concord. During the night, British troops crossed Boston Harbor into the Massachusetts countryside. American silversmith Paul Revere and many other riders warned the colonial militias and minutemen that the regulars—a term for the "regular" British Army—were coming.

The British regulars reached Lexington hungry and mud-covered after marching for nine hours. Few of the soldiers or officers expected a fight that day. The British did not capture Hancock or Adams, and they found little to destroy at Concord. At 5:00 a.m., they confronted members of the Lexington militia—a small group of just 74 men—on the town green. Someone fired the first shot, though no one knows who. Eight militiamen were killed and 10 were wounded.

Later that morning, in a fight over Concord's North Bridge, the colonists shot and killed two British soldiers. With the deaths of these men, the simmering rebellion erupted into war. American poet Ralph Waldo Emerson later called the death of the first British soldier "the shot heard round the world." By day's end, the fighting escalated into a running battle along the roads back to Boston.

More than 4,000 militias from at least 23 towns had swarmed to the scene of battle that day, including minutemen, a subset of the militia paid extra by their towns to be ready "at a moment's warning." Their alarm and outrage at the day's events escalated the violence. Meanwhile, the British were reinforced by 1,100 more regulars. Total British casualties included 65 killed, 180 wounded, and 27 missing. Estimated militia casualties were 50 killed, 39 wounded, and 5 missing.

These musket flints were found on the spot where New England militia had gathered on April 19, 1775, to confront British troops on Concord Bridge.

Amos Doolittle's 1775 engraving accurately depicts Lexington Green, the Buckman Tavern behind it, and the disordered retreat of the Lexington militia. Doolittle exaggerated the control and discipline of the British regulars, who were described as breaking ranks and firing without orders. He created three additional scenes showing other moments from the battles.

Grenadier Captain William Crosbie of the 38th Regiment of Foot posed for this painting around 1774, shortly before he sailed to America. He fought on April 19, 1775.

This 1946 painting by Tom Lovell highlights the grueling labors of American officer Henry Knox as he and his troops transported 59 cannons to Washington's army.

From Bunker Hill to Canada

After Lexington and Concord, 18,000 New England militiamen fought British regulars for control of Boston. Congress designated the volunteer troops around Boston the "Continental Army," signaling that the conflict was not limited to New England. Congress also appointed Virginia's George Washington as commander in chief and authorized reinforcements from the Mid-Atlantic and southern colonies.

In May 1775, Benedict Arnold and Ethan Allen led American militiamen in a surprise attack on Fort Ticonderoga in northern New York as part of a larger plan to retake Boston. The American troops defeated the small British garrison and captured the fort's heavy weaponry.

June 17, 1775, was the bloodiest day of the war. British commanders discovered that Americans had fortified Charlestown Peninsula, a hilly area with a commanding view of Boston. At the Battle of Bunker Hill, British troops drove the Americans out of their fort and burned the nearby town of Charlestown. Both sides suffered heavy casualties.

In November, General Washington assigned Henry Knox to bring him the captured guns at Fort Ticonderoga. Knox hoped "in 16 or 17 days to be able to present your Excellency a noble train of artillery." Instead, it took him 10 grueling weeks. His troops carried the 59 cannons over 300 miles on flat-bottomed boats and heavy sleds, across frozen lakes and through deep snow. In early March 1776, the troops dragged the cannons onto Dorchester and Roxbury Heights and finally forced the British to abandon Boston.

While Washington worked to recapture Boston, the Continental Army turned its eye toward Canada. American forces attacked Quebec City on December 31, 1775, in hopes of making the province of Quebec part of its alliance. The invasion of Canada displayed Americans' confidence in their cause. However, the Americans quickly discovered that the inhabitants of French-speaking Quebec were skeptical of invaders. Many still hoped for a return of French power, while others distrusted the New Englanders more than their English occupiers.

The Americans failed to wrest the city from British control in that assault or in the six-month siege that followed. By the end of June 1776, the Continental troops had all retreated from Canada, with British forces in pursuit.

Immediately after the Battle of Bunker Hill, Francis Medfield wrote in this 1755 Bible, thanking God for sparing his life.

In this 1786 depiction of the tragic death of General Montgomery during the assault on Quebec, John Trumbull shows Americans from different regions united around their fallen commander.

An Army Takes Shape

When General Washington took command of the Continental Army in early July 1775, the New England troops had been in the field for nearly three months. To the aristocratic Virginian, these Yankees were "an exceedingly dirty and nasty people." The soldiers of the Continental Army hailed from different regions, with sharply contrasting traditions, faiths, and opinions. Washington struggled to keep the peace among his troops. He also had to adjust to commanding men dedicated to different military traditions—and ideas of individual liberty.

New Englanders differed from their southern and Mid-Atlantic counterparts in many ways. In religion, they were predominantly Congregationalist, whereas troops from the South tended to be Presbyterian or Anglican. Many New England regiments included African Americans and American Indians in their ranks (hundreds of African American men served in 1775). This was less common among the southern corps. Yankee officers also tended to live, work, and play alongside their men, which some southerners considered a sign of a dangerous social equality.

Joining the New England troops were nine companies of expert riflemen from Pennsylvania, Maryland, and Virginia. Armed with highly accurate rifles, the men were legendary for their marksmanship. This reputation for accuracy had great propaganda value—the British press quickly shared accounts of unfortunate officers shot from great distances. Self-sufficient and individualistic, these troops wore distinctive clothing derived from frontier hunters' dress.

While initially hopeful about the riflemen's service, Washington quickly grew frustrated by their resistance to military discipline. In addition, these men often quarreled with their New England counterparts. Many New Englanders considered the riflemen's fringed hunting shirts a sign of their wearers' "savagery," while the riflemen distrusted the New Englanders' foreign ways.

The troops clashed in many ways, but together they were an army of ordinary people, fighting for their rights against the most powerful empire in the history of the world.

Massachusetts officer Benjamin Holden wore this uniform coat, top, during the Revolutionary War. Southern soldiers wore hunting shirts, like this one, to intimidate the enemy.

BEHIND THE SCENES

A host of experts created the Museum's collection of life-sized tableaus. The curatorial staff at the Museum worked closely with StudioEIS, one of the nation's leading design studios, as well as with professional sculptors, wigmakers, painters, and 18th-century costume specialists to construct historically accurate, realistic figures.

George Washington

From his childhood, George Washington aspired to be a British military hero. At 20, he became an officer in Virginia's colonial forces. He gained the favor of British General Edward Braddock, holding Braddock as he died at the Battle of the Monongahela in 1755. Later Washington served as the lieutenant colonel and then colonel of the Virginia Regiment during the French and Indian War.

Congress recognized Washington's experience as well as the advantages of appointing a Virginian in convincing Southern colonies to support the fight against Britain. Washington protested that he did not feel "equal to the extensive and important trust." But his combined physical strength and mastery of civility and refinement diffused conflicts within the army, making him the unifying figure for the Revolutionary cause.

Great Union Flag

1776, some Americans
a new flag. It expressed
for colonial unity, while
identify their struggle
store their British liberties.

This "Great Union" (or simply "Union")
flag combined the traditional British
Union in the upper canton with a
field of thirteen alternating red and
white stripes representing the thirteen
United Colonies.

A Brawl in Harvard Yard

In the first American army, troops from New England sometimes fought alongside soldiers recruited from the Pennsylvania, Maryland, and Virginia mountains. At other times, these troops fought each other. Eleven-year-old Israel Trask saw George Washington leap into one of these fights between American soldiers. The general pulled the men apart and tried to restore order in the camp.

The New Englanders in the fight included the sailing men of Marblehead. Trask thought these rough-and-tumble men of the coastal frontier were "full of fun and mischief." This Marblehead regiment, like the crew of many a New England ship, included African Americans. It is possible that the royal governor of Virginia's recruitment of enslaved people elevated the tensions in this desegregated force.

Joseph Brant, an experienced Iroquois Indian commander, helped persuade three of the six Iroquois nations—the Seneca, Cayuga, and his own Mohawk people—to ally with the British.

Thomas Paine

Thomas Paine arrived in Philadelphia from England in 1774. Paine quickly took up the American cause, writing some of the most influential political essays of the American Revolution. At the beginning of 1776, Paine's pamphlet *Common Sense*—which sold thousands of copies in its first few months—inspired Americans to declare independence. In an appendix to *Common Sense*, he encouraged Americans, stating, "We have it in our power to begin the world over again."

Paine joined the Continental Army, retreating through New Jersey with Washington's ragged army in December 1776. He recalled that in a "passion of patriotism," he wrote a new pamphlet, *The American Crisis No. I*. It stirred Americans to regroup, reenlist, and fight again.

Revolution

Everything changed in 1776. Up to this point, Americans fought for their rights within the British empire, but now Americans declared themselves independent of Great Britain. They radically rejected not only King George, but also the whole idea of rule by a monarch. From here forward, Americans fought for republicanism—the idea that the people should control their own governments. They believed American colonies must separate from Britain and create independent states. They called their movement a revolution. By this, they meant a new turn in history, a new way of looking at the world.

The King responded to their uprising with ferocity. He stated that the colonists were engaged in rebellion and sedition; his former subjects were now his enemies. Swiftly, King George emptied Britain's castles of soldiers and hired foreign mercenaries in Germany, dispatching a massive armada from Great Britain to arrive in New York.

Not everyone in the colonies supported the Revolution, though. Across America, many men and women who proclaimed their support for independence clashed with neighbors, friends, and family members who remained loyal to the King. Most Loyalists—American supporters of the King—saw independence as a reckless "leap in the dark." In their view, the British Empire was still the greatest in history. It provided more liberty for ordinary people than any other power in Europe. Why discard all that for new governments run by nobodies, with no credit and no armies? Loyalists believed that those who took up arms and defended King George III would later be remembered as heroes.

Both Loyalists and Revolutionaries terrorized those who refused to take sides. Native American nations faced losing their independence. Enslaved African Americans sought power to protect and perhaps free themselves from the violence of war. Neutrals found their lands confiscated and property destroyed. Perhaps because of these terrors, many people who did not wish to be involved in the war ended up having to choose a side.

Did You Know?

Perhaps the earliest use of the term American Revolution appeared in several 1776 speeches and publications by South Carolinian William Henry Drayton. Drayton argued that the King had abandoned his people and that the American Revolution would set them free. He believed that this was the dawn of a new age in world history.

First published in January 1776, Thomas Paine's *Common Sense* urged Americans to declare independence. The Loyalist pamphlet *Plain Truth* appeared that spring. It aimed to dismantle Paine's arguments.

Declaring Independence

Abigail Adams wrote to her congressman husband, John, in March 1776, stating that the King's abuses proved that men were tyrants. Only the influence of women, she said, could secure reason and liberty.

For months across the colonies, many voices had been clamoring for independence. In June 1776, the Second Continental Congress met in the State House (Independence Hall) in Philadelphia to debate the issue. Those opposed were in the minority. They pleaded for more time, hoping that despite the open warfare, the colonies could still reconcile with the mother country.

The debate continued until July 2, 1776, when Congress declared the United States independent. Two days later, it issued the Declaration of Independence to explain its break from Great Britain. Crowds rejoiced as copies of the Declaration were read aloud in town squares across the newly declared states and published in newspapers around the world.

The Declaration of Independence announced the birth of the United States, dissolving royal authority, but it did not create a system of government. To reestablish law in America, 11 of the 13 states had begun writing constitutions prior to July 1776. Meanwhile, eight days after issuing the Declaration, Congress debated the Articles of Confederation, which outlined a system of national government.

Although the authors of the Declaration of Independence stated that "all men are created equal," most of them probably never imagined their words would inspire calls for equality from women, slaves, and the poor. But that is what happened. Most of the states lowered the amount of property a man had to own to qualify to vote. Abigail Adams asserted women's right to a voice in government. And between 1776 and 1804, every state north of Maryland began the process of ending slavery. Even in Virginia and the Carolinas, the moral acceptability of slavery was questioned as never before.

The new republican governments in America also experimented with religious freedom. In its 1776 constitution, Pennsylvania invoked religious freedom. Maryland eliminated from its state constitution the requirement that voters and officeholders needed to be Protestant. In Virginia, Thomas Jefferson adapted the state's laws to guarantee religious freedom.

The Declaration's promises were far-reaching—and have been expanding ever since.

Independence Hall, then called the State House, was the nation's capitol, where the Continental Congress debated and voted for independence.

IN CONGRESS, JULY 4, 1776.

A DECLARATION

BY THE REPRESENTATIVES OF THE

UNITED STATES OF AMERICA,

IN GENERAL CONGRESS ASSEMBLED.

WHEN in the Course of human Events, it becomes necessary for one People to dissolve the Political Bands which have connected them with another, and to assume among the Powers of the Earth, the separate and equal Station to which the Laws of Nature and of Nature's God entitle them, a decent Respect to the Opinions of Mankind requires that they should declare the causes which impel them to the Separation.

We hold these Truths to be self-evident, that all Men are created equal, that they are endowed by their Creator with certain unalienable Rights, that among these are Life, Liberty, and the Pursuit of Happiness——That to secure these Rights, Governments are instituted among Men, deriving their just Powers from the Consent of the Governed, that whenever any Form of Government becomes destructive of these Ends, it is the Right of the People to alter or to abolish it, and to institute new Government, laying its Foundation on such Principles, and organizing its Powers in such Form, as to them shall seem most likely to effect their Safety and Happiness. Prudence, indeed, will dictate that Governments long established should not be changed for light and transient Causes; and accordingly all Experience hath shewn, that Mankind are more disposed to suffer, while Evils are sufferable, than to right themselves by abolishing the Forms to which they are accustomed. But when a long Train of Abuses and Usurpations, pursuing invariably the same Object, evinces a Design to reduce them under absolute Despotism, it is their Right, it is their Duty, to throw off such Government, and to provide new Guards for their future Security. Such has been the patient Sufferance of these Colonies; and such is now the Necessity which constrains them to alter their former Systems of Government. The History of the present King of Great-Britain is a History of repeated Injuries and Usurpations, all having in direct Object the Establishment of an absolute Tyranny over these States. To prove this, let Facts be submitted to a candid World.

He has refused his Assent to Laws, the most wholesome and necessary for the public Good.

He has forbidden his Governors to pass Laws of immediate and pressing Importance, unless suspended in their Operation till his Assent should be obtained; and when so suspended, he has utterly neglected to attend to them.

He has refused to pass other Laws for the Accommodation of large Districts of People, unless those People would relinquish the Right of Representation in the Legislature, a Right inestimable to them, and formidable to Tyrants only.

He has called together Legislative Bodies at Places unusual, uncomfortable, and distant from the Depository of their public Records, for the sole Purpose of fatiguing them into Compliance with his Measures.

He has dissolved Representative Houses repeatedly, for opposing with manly Firmness his Invasions on the Rights of the People.

He has refused for a long Time, after such Dissolutions, to cause others to be elected; whereby the Legislative Powers, incapable of Annihilation, have returned to the People at large for their exercise; the State remaining in the mean time exposed to all the Dangers of Invasion from without, and Convulsions within.

He has endeavoured to prevent the Population of these States; for that Purpose obstructing the Laws for Naturalization of Foreigners; refusing to pass others to encourage their Migrations hither, and raising the Conditions of new Appropriations of Lands.

He has obstructed the Administration of Justice, by refusing his Assent to Laws for establishing Judiciary Powers.

He has made Judges dependent on his Will alone, for the Tenure of their Offices, and the Amount and Payment of their Salaries.

He has erected a Multitude of new Offices, and sent hither Swarms of Officers to harrass our People, and eat out their Substance.

He has kept among us, in Times of Peace, Standing Armies, without the consent of our Legislatures.

He has affected to render the Military independent of and superior to the Civil Power.

He has combined with others to subject us to a Jurisdiction foreign to our Constitution, and unacknowledged by our Laws; giving his Assent to their Acts of pretended Legislation:

For quartering large Bodies of Armed Troops among us:

For protecting them, by a mock Trial, from Punishment for any Murders which they should commit on the Inhabitants of these States:

For cutting off our Trade with all Parts of the World:

For imposing Taxes on us without our Consent:

For depriving us, in many Cases, of the Benefits of Trial by Jury:

For transporting us beyond Seas to be tried for pretended Offences:

For abolishing the free System of English Laws in a neighbouring Province, establishing therein an arbitrary Government, and enlarging its Boundaries, so as to render it at once an Example and fit Instrument for introducing the same absolute Rule into these Colonies:

For taking away our Charters, abolishing our most valuable Laws, and altering fundamentally the Forms of our Governments:

For suspending our own Legislatures, and declaring themselves invested with Power to legislate for us in all Cases whatsoever.

He has abdicated Government here, by declaring us out of his Protection and waging War against us.

He has plundered our Seas, ravaged our Coasts, burnt our Towns, and destroyed the Lives of our People.

He is, at this Time, transporting large Armies of foreign Mercenaries to compleat the Works of Death, Desolation, and Tyranny, already begun with circumstances of Cruelty and Perfidy, scarcely paralleled in the most barbarous Ages, and totally unworthy the Head of a civilized Nation.

He has constrained our fellow Citizens taken Captive on the high Seas to bear Arms against their Country, to become the Executioners of their Friends and Brethren, or to fall themselves by their Hands.

He has excited domestic Insurrections amongst us, and has endeavoured to bring on the Inhabitants of our Frontiers, the merciless Indian Savages, whose known Rule of Warfare, is an undistinguished Destruction, of all Ages, Sexes and Conditions.

In every stage of these Oppressions we have Petitioned for Redress in the most humble Terms: Our repeated Petitions have been answered only by repeated Injury. A Prince, whose Character is thus marked by every act which may define a Tyrant, is unfit to be the Ruler of a free People.

Nor have we been wanting in Attentions to our British Brethren. We have warned them from Time to Time of Attempts by their Legislature to extend an unwarrantable Jurisdiction over us. We have reminded them of the Circumstances of our Emigration and Settlement here. We have appealed to their native Justice and Magnanimity, and we have conjured them by the Ties of our common Kindred to disavow these Usurpations, which, would inevitably interrupt our Connections and Correspondence. They too have been deaf to the Voice of Justice and of Consanguinity. We must, therefore, acquiesce in the Necessity, which denounces our Separation, and hold them, as we hold the rest of Mankind, Enemies in War, in Peace, Friends.

We, therefore, the Representatives of the UNITED STATES OF AMERICA, in GENERAL CONGRESS, Assembled, appealing to the Supreme Judge of the World for the Rectitude of our Intentions, do, in the Name, and by Authority of the good People of these Colonies, solemnly Publish and Declare, That these United Colonies are, and of Right ought to be, FREE AND INDEPENDENT STATES; that they are absolved from all Allegiance to the British Crown, and that all political Connection between them and the State of Great-Britain, is and ought to be totally dissolved; and that as FREE AND INDEPENDENT STATES, they have full Power to levy War, conclude Peace, contract Alliances, establish Commerce, and to do all other Acts and Things which INDEPENDENT STATES may of right do. And for the support of this Declaration, with a firm Reliance on the Protection of divine Providence, we mutually pledge to each other our Lives, our Fortunes, and our sacred Honor.

Signed by ORDER and in BEHALF of the CONGRESS,

JOHN HANCOCK, PRESIDENT.

ATTEST.

CHARLES THOMSON, SECRETARY.

PHILADELPHIA: PRINTED BY JOHN DUNLAP.

John Dunlap printed the first copies of the Declaration of Independence on July 4, 1776. The Declaration justified Congress's actions with a list of 27 charges against King George III.

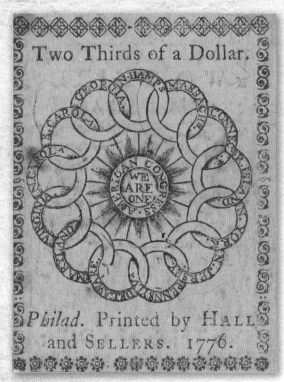

The chain of interlocking states, designed by Benjamin Franklin, came to symbolize the United States. The design first appeared on paper money on February 17, 1776.

Did You Know?

The first foreign language the Declaration of Independence was translated into was German for the large Pennsylvania German population. This translation was printed four days after the first English printings of the Declaration were available in the Philadelphia newspaper Der Pennsylvanischer Staatsbote.

THE

CONSTITUTION

OF THE

Commonwealth of Pennsylvania,

AS ESTABLISHED BY THE

GENERAL CONVENTION.

CAREFULLY COMPARED WITH THE ORIGINAL.

TO WHICH IS ADDED,

A

REPORT OF THE COMMITTEE

APPOINTED TO ENQUIRE,

" Whether the Constitution has been preserved inviolate in every Part, and
" whether the legislative and executive Branches of Government, have per-
" formed their Duty as Guardians of the People, or assumed to themselves,
" or exercised other or greater Powers, than they are intitled to by the
" Constitution."

AS ADOPTED BY THE

COUNCIL OF CENSORS.

Published by their Order.

PHILADELPHIA:

PRINTED BY FRANCIS BAILEY, AT YORICK'S HEAD,
IN MARKET-STREET.
M.DCC.LXXXIV.

Of all the Revolutionary state constitutions, the Pennsylvania constitution of September 1776 gave the most power to "the people."

The final Great Seal of the United States was adopted by Congress in 1782. It featured a bald eagle clutching an olive branch and arrows as symbols of peace and war. The reverse included a pyramid with an all-seeing eye.

Probably made by an American POW for his sweetheart, this busk, a woman's accessory, is decorated with Revolutionary symbols.

Mumbet

Known as Mumbet, Elizabeth Freeman lived as a slave in Massachusetts. One morning after she heard the Declaration of Independence read, she announced that its promise of equality should include her. Her master hit her with a fire shovel. She did what Yankees do—she got a lawyer—and won her freedom in court. Her case set a precedent prohibiting slavery in Massachusetts. She later stated, "Any time while I was a slave, if one minute's freedom had been offered to me, and I had been told I must die at the end of that minute, I would have taken it—just to stand one minute on God's earth a free woman—I would."

Tearing Down King George III

General George Washington ordered that the Declaration of Independence be read to the army in New York City. The troops were supposed to return to their quarters afterward, but some soldiers and sailors took to the streets. Near the waterfront, the mob tore down the statue of King George III and smashed it into pieces.

Beneath its gilt finish, the statue was made of 4,000 pounds of lead. Revolutionaries hacked up the King and his horse and hauled the dismembered statue to Litchfield, Connecticut. There, women and children melted it down into more than 42,000 musket balls. Loyalists quietly recovered the King's head and smuggled it to England. Only a few fragments, including the ones displayed at the Museum, survived.

Published in Paris, this print (circa 1778) depicts New York City on September 20, 1776, when wind-blown flames destroyed a quarter of the British-controlled city.

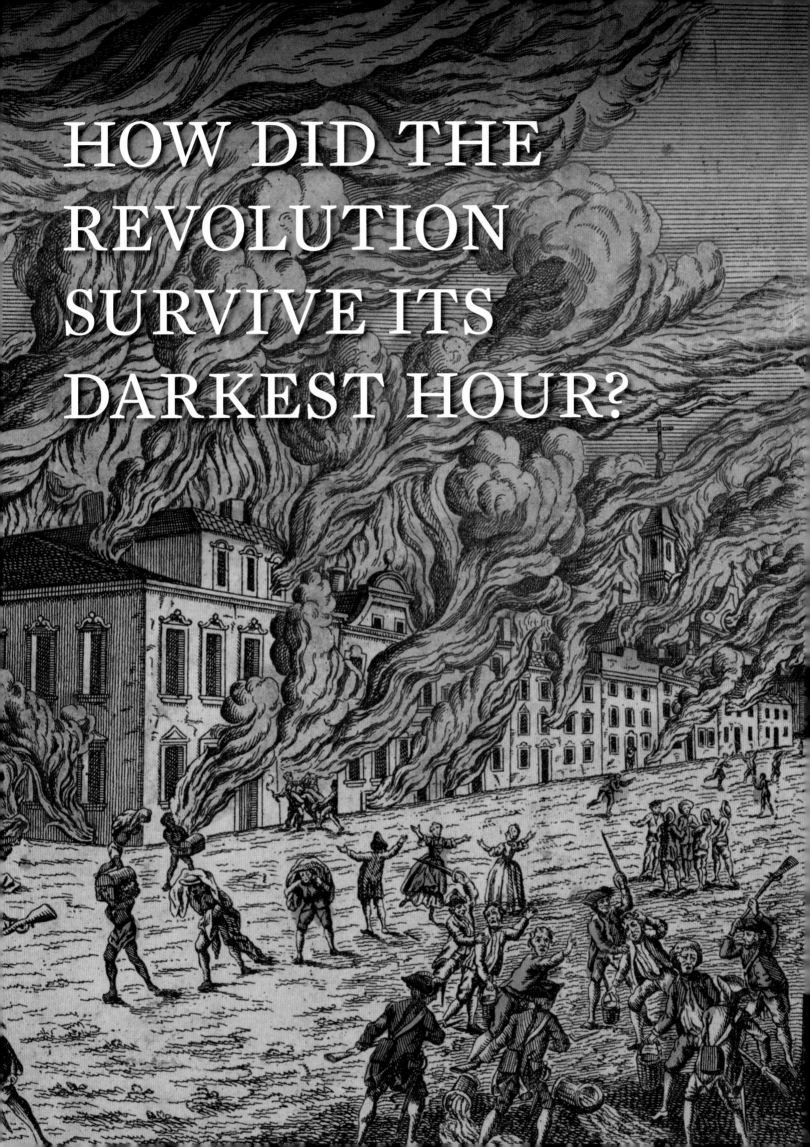

HOW DID THE REVOLUTION SURVIVE ITS DARKEST HOUR?

Alonzo Chappel realistically portrayed the chaos of battle in his paintings. In this circa-1858 image of the Battle of Long Island, Chappel focused on the panic of the Connecticut men.

that I ever saw discharged in anger."

WILLIAM BURKE

William Burke

Private William Burke had never heard a shot fired in anger until he came to America. The 24-year-old Irishman joined the British 45th Regiment of Foot in 1774. In 1775, he crossed the Atlantic Ocean to Boston, part of the force sent to punish that city for the Tea Party. Like many British soldiers, he was bilingual. He spoke both English and Irish Gaelic. Others spoke Scottish, Welsh, German, or various dialects of those languages. Private Burke did not see combat until he reached New York in 1776. Many years later, he described America as a place of "trouble and sorrow."

Battle for New York

With the ink barely dry on the Declaration of Independence, Americans faced the wrath of King George III. The Battle of Long Island began on August 27, part of the King's attempt to seize New York. Outnumbered, the majority of American troops escaped to Manhattan. The British then attacked Manhattan Island on September 15, 1776, with an amphibious landing at Kip's Bay. Amphibious landings allowed the massive firepower of the British ships to provide cover for the attacking infantry.

The British hammered the Americans for more than an hour with a barrage of cannon fire from five warships. Then 4,000 British and Hessian soldiers in 80 flat-boats landed to finish the assault. The troops aboard these vessels numbered around 32,000 soldiers.

Only a few hundred Connecticut soldiers guarded the shore with nothing but a poorly made wall of sand to protect them. The American troops ran, retreating until they reached the Harlem Highlands on the north side of Manhattan.

The Continental Army, barely a year old, was fighting the most powerful and professional army and navy in Europe. Americans believed they would triumph against the odds, since they were fighting for a noble cause. But the campaign of 1776 in New York and New Jersey tested that faith.

The battles moved from south to north, with General Sir William Howe's British forces constantly outmaneuvering and overwhelming Washington's army. The British aimed to divide New England (which they believed was the most rebellious region) from the Mid-Atlantic and the south. In four months of fighting—August to November 1776—the British and Hessian troops took control of Long Island, Manhattan Island (including New York City), Staten Island, and the Hudson Valley.

November 1776 ended with the Continental Army retreating for its life across New Jersey. Washington wrote that he had "not above 3,000 men, and they very much broken and dispirited." The troops under his direct command had dwindled by 80 percent due to desertions, expiring enlistments, and the extension of his army over a larger area.

By early December, Washington's beleaguered troops still remained only a few steps ahead of British General Charles Cornwallis. But in this, the darkest moment of the war so far, the ragged veterans of the New York campaign finally found hope as reinforcements began to arrive from Pennsylvania.

Toys like this ceramic lamb were excavated from a British Revolutionary War campsite around New York City. They are reminders that the families of British soldiers accompanied the army in America.

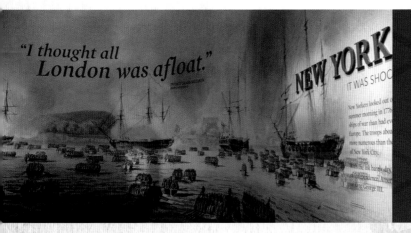

"I thought all London was afloat."

BEHIND **THE SCENES**

To highlight the drama of King George's impending attack on Kip's Bay, Museum curators enlarged a 17.5-by-26-inch watercolor painting, *The British Landing at Kip's Bay, New York Island, 15 September 1776.* This 1700s image, painted by British officer Robert Cleveley, was reproduced at 19 feet tall by 29 feet wide.

In 1776, brothers Admiral Richard Howe (shown here) and General Sir William Howe commanded the British Navy and Army in America.

The Forster Flag was one of the earliest British flags converted to an American flag after the Declaration of Independence.

Colonel John Chandler of Connecticut carried this small sword, circa 1690–1710, during the Revolutionary War.

Americans wore their causes. They emblazoned their hats and equipment with patriotic and republican words and symbols.

Many soldiers' families lived and traveled with them. This circa-1780 image shows a typical British camp in England. British camps in America looked similar.

Joseph Plumb Martin

Private Joseph Plumb Martin was one of thousands of teenaged soldiers in Washington's Continental Army. In June 1776, he left his beloved "grandsire's" farm in Milford, Connecticut, and joined the army in New York City. On the morning of August 27, 1776, one of Martin's officers announced that the British were attacking Long Island and that Martin and his fellow fledgling soldiers were going to have to "snuff a little gunpowder." Martin also experienced the attack on Kip's Bay. He remembered that the redcoats were so thick that "they appeared like a large field of clover in bloom." Vastly overpowered, Martin and his fellow Americans ran.

Answering the Call

This canteen is inscribed with the name "Asaph Parmele," who served with the 13th Regiment of Connecticut Militia.

Those who wished to serve the cause of liberty could join units organized by Congress, by the states, or by local authorities. Congress authorized Continental regiments. Soldiers served for at least a year and had to accept strict army hierarchy and discipline.

Levy units were raised by the states for periods of between three and nine months to reinforce the Continental Army. Militias were authorized by the states but raised by local authorities. Militia service was required in many states, including those in New England, but voluntary in some, like Pennsylvania.

Many of the reinforcements for Washington's retreating army were volunteer militiamen from Pennsylvania. Known as the Associators, these men had been strong advocates of American independence and their state's democratic constitution of 1776.

The Pennsylvania Associators applied the principle of consent of the governed to their recruitment practices. They followed many of the republican practices of the Revolutionary state constitutions. They elected their officers and even voted on what uniforms and equipment to wear.

In December 1776, the Pennsylvania Associators answered calls from General Washington and Congress to reinforce the Continental Army. Washington's dwindling forces had taken refuge on the west side of the Delaware, where the river created a natural barricade between themselves and Cornwallis's British Army in New Jersey.

The first Associators reached the Continental Army on December 5. Over the next three weeks, more volunteers arrived from all over Pennsylvania and Delaware. Despite the army's growing numbers, it wasn't clear whether these troops would be enough to halt the British advance.

Howard Pyle's 1898 painting, *Retreat through the Jerseys*, captures Washington's ragged troops at the end of 1776.

"*These are the times that try men's souls. The summer soldier and the sunshine patriot will, in this crisis, shrink from the service of their country; but he that stands by it now, deserves the love and thanks of man and woman. Tyranny, like hell, is not easily conquered; yet we have this consolation with us, that the harder the conflict, the more glorious the triumph.*"

—THOMAS PAINE, *The American Crisis No. 1*

Colonel Benjamin Flower is shown in the splendid uniform of an artillery officer, including symbols of his rank and patriotic support.

Jonathan Pettibone

French and Indian War veteran Colonel Jonathan Pettibone carried a silver-hilted sword engraved with his name when he commanded the 18th Connecticut Militia Regiment in 1776. From their positions in Manhattan, the Connecticut militiamen could hear raging cannon and gunfire as the Battle of Brooklyn Heights began on August 27. Colonel Pettibone fell ill in September and died in Rye, New York, on his march home. In his will, Pettibone left his sword to his son Jonathan, who also served in the militia.

A man staggere
clothes. He was
face full of sores

he was not

Only when

brother Jam

Two Brothers Face the Darkest Days of the Revolutionary War

Lieutenant Charles Willson Peale belonged to a Philadelphia Associator company. On December 8, 1776, he was part of the reinforcements for Washington's Continental Army. His brother, Ensign James Peale, had served as an officer through the long New York campaign. He was one of the few who had survived the retreat through New Jersey.

The brothers reunited on the banks of the Delaware River in Pennslyvania. James was ragged, with a long beard and a face full of sores. Charles later wrote, "Only when he spoke did I recognize my brother James."

Both brothers were portrait artists after the war. Charles Willson Peale painted the reunification scene for Thomas Jefferson, but the work was lost. He included "a female figure with two children" as a testament to the sacrifices and patriotism of camp followers.

of line and came toward me. He had lost
old dirty blanket jacket, his beard long and his
so disfigured him that

wn by me on first sight.
poke did I recognize my

CHARLES WILLSON PEALE

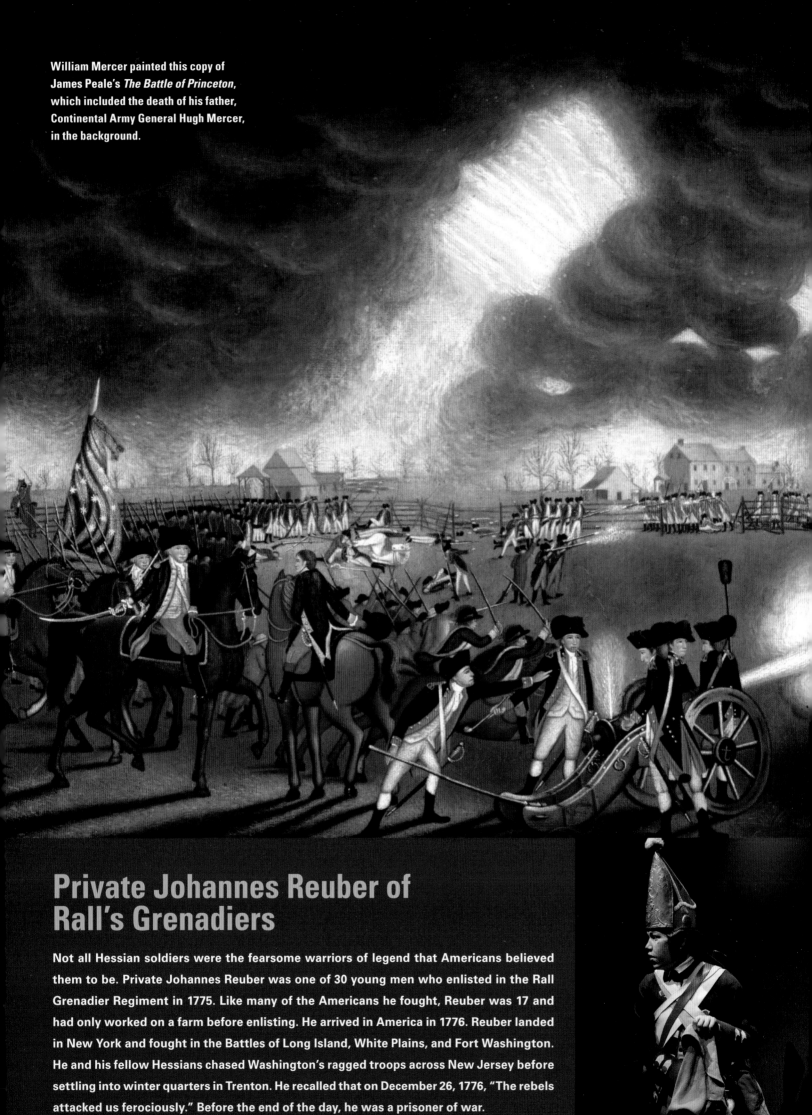

William Mercer painted this copy of James Peale's *The Battle of Princeton*, which included the death of his father, Continental Army General Hugh Mercer, in the background.

Private Johannes Reuber of Rall's Grenadiers

Not all Hessian soldiers were the fearsome warriors of legend that Americans believed them to be. Private Johannes Reuber was one of 30 young men who enlisted in the Rall Grenadier Regiment in 1775. Like many of the Americans he fought, Reuber was 17 and had only worked on a farm before enlisting. He arrived in America in 1776. Reuber landed in New York and fought in the Battles of Long Island, White Plains, and Fort Washington. He and his fellow Hessians chased Washington's ragged troops across New Jersey before settling into winter quarters in Trenton. He recalled that on December 26, 1776, "The rebels attacked us ferociously." Before the end of the day, he was a prisoner of war.

Washington's Gamble

In December 1776, Washington took a desperate gamble. Across the Delaware River from his Continental Army, a small garrison of Hessians had taken up winter quarters in Trenton, New Jersey. The Hessians, considered some of the fiercest soldiers in the world, were Germans hired by King George III to defeat the Revolutionaries. Their tall brass caps and sharp uniforms contrasted with the American soldiers' rags.

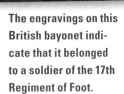

The Hessians expected little threat from Washington's beleaguered army. They would pay dearly for underestimating the Revolutionaries. On Christmas night and the following morning, Washington crossed the Delaware into New Jersey—marching for miles in the severe cold—and captured the garrison of Hessians at Trenton in under 45 minutes. He sent the 900 Hessian prisoners to Philadelphia under guard.

The engravings on this British bayonet indicate that it belonged to a soldier of the 17th Regiment of Foot.

Washington then crossed his troops back to Pennsylvania. Unaware of Washington's decision to return to Pennsylvania, General John Cadwalader of the Pennsylvania Associators crossed into New Jersey, accidentally isolating his troops from the main American force. Fortunately, he discovered that the Hessians had evacuated all of their Delaware River posts. With no apparent counterattack looming, Washington decided to retake Trenton and recrossed the Delaware a third time.

On January 1, news reached Washington that General Cornwallis was gathering 8,000 British troops in Princeton, New Jersey. Washington concentrated his 6,000 troops in Trenton. Hundreds of soon-to-be-discharged Continentals volunteered to serve for two more weeks.

As he lay dying at the Battle of Princeton, General Hugh Mercer defended himself against the bayonet attacks of the 17th Regiment with this sword.

On January 2, American guards skirmished with General Cornwallis's troops along the road between Princeton and Trenton. At dusk, Cornwallis reached Trenton, where the armies engaged in heavy street fighting. As night fell, Cornwallis encamped near Assunpink Bridge, confident of victory the next day.

Rather than continue the fight in Trenton, Washington snuck away and boldly counterattacked the British rear guard, striking just south of Princeton at dawn on January 3. After a hard fight, the exhausted American troops captured the town. Washington then marched north to build winter quarters in the New Jersey Highlands. In these 10 short days, General Washington and his army saved the Revolutionary War effort and perhaps the cause of American independence itself.

Revolutionary War veteran and American artist John Trumbull painted the surrender of Hessian General Johann Rall to George Washington at Trenton. Mortally wounded, Rall died hours after his surrender.

Washington's War Tent

In this circa 1780–90 print, General Washington stands outside his tent holding the Declaration of Independence. Shredded documents of the colonies' efforts to reconcile with Britain are strewn on the ground.

Washington's men were supposed to form a "continental" army. Comprised of New England farmers and fishermen, hunters from Pennsylvania and Virginia, these soldiers distrusted one another almost as much as they did the British—but Washington knew he must unite them.

He prepared the army, and himself, knowing the war could be a long one: "After I have once got into a Tent," he wrote in 1776, "I shall not soon quit it." He kept his promise. Through the entire war, Washington saw his Virginia home of Mount Vernon for only a few days. Washington's tent served as his private office, becoming both his home and headquarters. There, he sat alone, reading and writing the letters that marked the highest and lowest moments of the war.

At the end of the war, Washington halted a conspiracy by recalling the many sacrifices he'd made for the Revolution. In 1783, when officers at Newburgh, New York, cursed Congress and spoke of making Washington a ruler or king, the commander in chief confronted them: "I have never left your side one moment. I have been the constant companion and witness to your distresses. I have not only grown gray, but almost blind in the service of my country." By reminding them of the cause that kept them together in the "tented field," he may have saved the republic.

After the war, Washington's tent was passed down through Martha Washington's family to her great-granddaughter, Mary Custis Lee, the wife of Confederate General Robert E. Lee. During the Civil War, when Union troops occupied Arlington, the Lees' home, an enslaved woman named Selina Gray was left as caretaker of Arlington and the Washington relics. The tent was removed from Arlington and placed on exhibit in the nation's capital for the Union cause. In 1901, it was finally returned to Mary Custis Lee, daughter of Robert E. and Mary Custis Lee, who sold it in 1909 to raise money for the care of Confederate widows.

Reverend W. Herbert Burk bought the tent in hopes of building a museum to honor Washington and the American Revolution. The Museum acquired Reverend Burk's collection in 2003. Today, Washington's tent survives as a symbol of the fragile American experiment—the power of the people to secure their own freedoms.

BEHIND THE SCENES

Textile conservator Virginia Whelan, assisted by Joanna Hurd (not pictured), spent more than 500 hours preparing Washington's tent for display at the Museum. Whelan affixed transparent netting atop and beneath approximately 550 holes to stabilize the tent. For bigger tears and holes, she printed high-resolution images on polyester to graft into the original fabric.

This 1911 postcard is from a photograph Reverend Burk took of the tent shortly after the Valley Forge Historical Society acquired it.

William Lee

Although George Washington was a champion of liberty, he was also a slaveholder. William Lee, his valet (or manservant), was one of hundreds of thousands of African Americans held in bondage in the emerging nation. In 1775, Lee joined his master on the battlefield, caring for Washington's horses and other possessions and helping with his master's personal matters. After the war, Lee followed Washington back to Mount Vernon and attended the Constitutional Convention with Washington in 1787. Washington freed Lee in his last will and testament, stating that Lee could remain in Washington's service "if he should prefer it." Washington gave Lee an annuity of $30 for "his faithful services during the Revolutionary War."

George Washington's field tent likely was made in Reading, Pennsylvania, in early 1778, while he encamped at Valley Forge.

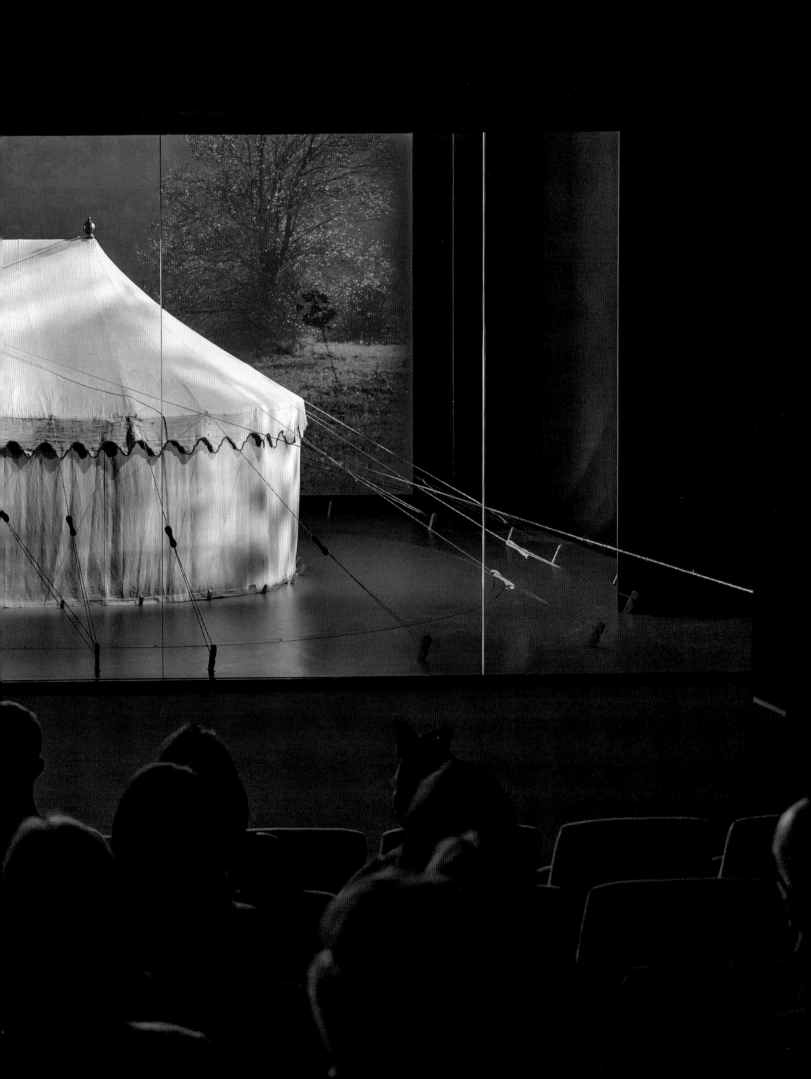

During the Revolutionary War, Native Americans had to choose the best strategy for safeguarding their homes and lands.

The Oneida Decision

Every Oneida, from chiefs to warriors to clan mothers, debated whether or not to ally with the Americans. The Museum's Oneida Nation Theater captures that moment, showcasing several Oneida figures—Skenandoah, Wá:li, Grasshopper, Han Yerry, Paul Powless, and Two Kettles—debate the future of the Oneida and the Haudenosaunee Confederacy.

Native Americans Choose Sides

The Revolutionary War divided more than just the colonists. Many Native American nations, like the Oneida, were also pressured to choose sides.

Many centuries before, the Oneida ancestors and the Mohawk, Onondaga, Cayuga, and Seneca nations had fought each other. By the 1100s, these five nations were living under the Great Law of Peace. They had buried their weapons and created an Iroquois Confederacy of nations. (A sixth nation, the Tuscarora, joined the Iroquois Confederacy in 1722.)

When the first battle of the Revolutionary War broke out in 1775, the Iroquois told their colonial brothers that the six nations would stand together—that unity was their strength. But after the colonists declared independence from King George, war threatened that peace.

The Iroquois Confederacy was divided. Some nations wished to stay neutral. They believed that King George and the colonists were like a parent and child and that they should stay out of the family quarrel. Some wanted to support the British and King George, who promised to protect their lands forever if they stood with him. And some wanted to support the new United States. They viewed the colonists as their neighbors and the British as the invaders. Ultimately, four of the six Iroquois nations actively sided with the British, while the Oneida and Tuscarora supported the Revolutionaries, joining the United States in its war.

In the 1730s, Lapowinsa and the Lenape were cheated by British officials and colonials. During the Revolution, some Lenape allied with the Americans, some with the British, and some tried to remain neutral.

Stockbridge warriors from Massachusetts often fought alongside New Englanders against the British.

On August 6, 1777, more than 60 Oneida fighters and patriot militiamen clashed with Iroquois warriors and Loyalists in the Battle of Oriskany, several miles from Fort Schuyler. It was one of the fiercest battles of the Revolutionary War. More than half a century later, an American Indian veteran remembered that blood ran along the ground like a stream.

On that tragic day, the Oneida stood alongside their new allies. And they have fought alongside American soldiers in every conflict since then.

> *"The disturbances in America give great trouble to all our nations, and many strange stories have been told to us by the people of that country."*
> —JOSEPH BRANT, 1776

The Baroness's Saratoga

In an extraordinary journal, the Baroness Von Riedesel wrote openly of the emotional and physical traumas she suffered on the Saratoga campaign.

For the British, the Saratoga campaign—which took place between June and October 1777—did not go according to plan.

British General John Burgoyne intended to crush the American Revolution by seizing the waterways between Quebec and New York City, effectively splitting troublesome New England from the rest of the rebel colonies and ending the war. Instead, the British lost two key battles at Saratoga, forcing Burgoyne to surrender to American General Horatio Gates on October 17, 1777.

The Baroness Von Riedesel was one of hundreds of women who followed the British Army to Saratoga. Her husband commanded the Brunswick (Hessian) troops in Burgoyne's army. The baroness, who with her three children accompanied her husband through the whole Saratoga campaign, left one of the finest accounts of the war from a woman's perspective.

On September 19, the baroness witnessed the baron's Brunswick troops fighting in the open fields of a local farm. On October 7, she heard the firing as they engaged with American troops under Benedict Arnold. She and her servants provided aid to badly wounded officers. In the final days of the siege, the baroness guarded the lives of many women, children, and wounded men, barricading them in a basement as American cannonballs slammed the house for six days. For most of this time, the firing was so heavy that they could not leave, and the basement filled with excrement. But she probably saved dozens of lives.

After the British surrendered, the baroness became a prisoner, along with her husband and nearly 5,000 British and Brunswick troops. To prevent their escape or rescue, Congress moved Burgoyne's captured army to Boston in 1777, then to Virginia in February 1779, and to Lancaster and York, Pennsylvania, in 1781. They were not freed until the war ended in 1783.

The Saratoga campaign did not grant Americans an immediate peace, but it did change the war. With the American victory, the French gained confidence to declare a formal military alliance with the United States—and the Revolutionaries found new hope.

Muskets used by the Americans between 1775 and 1777 are shown on the left of this display. On the right are types used later in the war, including some France provided.

James Peale painted General Horatio Gates, a former British officer-turned-Revolutionary, as he commanded the American forces at Saratoga. Gates had serious conflicts with his field commanders but was popular with New England militiamen.

After sailing his army up the Chesapeake Bay, British
General Sir William Howe (depicted circa 1777)
defeated the Americans at Brandywine in September
1777. Shortly afterward, he captured Philadelphia.
The British held the city until June 1778.

Philadelphia Falls

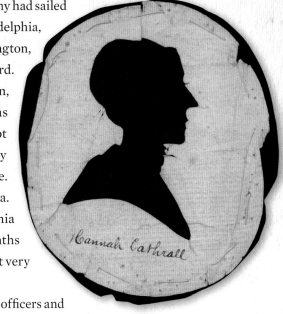

By the late summer of 1777, the British were on the move. General Howe's army had sailed from New York, landed in Maryland, and marched north to attack Philadelphia, the American capital. In his path was the Brandywine River. General Washington, seeking the advantage of higher ground, hoped to force the fight at Chadds Ford. But the British outflanked the Americans. Fighting took place all over the region, with one important battle occurring at Birmingham Meeting House, which was defended only by the men of the 3rd Virginia Regiment. Outnumbered but not outfought, the 3rd Virginia Regiment pinned the British troops down for nearly an hour, keeping General Howe's army from routing the entire American force.

Two weeks later, the British marched unopposed into the city of Philadelphia. Within hours of capturing Philadelphia, British troops seized the Pennsylvania State House (Independence Hall). The symbolism was profound: only 14 months earlier, the Continental Congress had voted for American independence in that very building.

Early in the occupation, Independence Hall served as a prison for American officers and a barracks for British soldiers. Most of the American prisoners in Independence Hall were from Virginia and Pennsylvania regiments. These men had been captured in the Battles of Brandywine and Germantown. Under close confinement on the upper floor of the State House, they suffered from hunger, cold, and battle wounds. British General Howe considered these harsh conditions to be retaliation for the American treatment of British prisoners.

Philadelphia women also suffered harsh conditions. Elizabeth Drinker, a Quaker, did not support the war. To help pay for the war, Revolutionaries confiscated some of her furniture. Later they held her husband as a Loyalist for several months. After the British arrived, she initially avoided housing officers in her home but ultimately had to. For many women, the war came into their homes.

Hannah Catherall, a Quaker schoolmistress, brought food and medicine to the wounded American prisoners in the Pennsylvania State House.

Independence Hall

During the early months of the British occupation, a detachment of British grenadiers lived in the lower level of the Pennsylvania State House (Independence Hall). Nearly 70 captured and wounded American officers were held on the floor above. Civilians who visited the prisoners were deeply affected by their suffering.

On October 8, 1777, schoolmistress Hannah Catherall was among a group of Quaker women who went to see the wounded American prisoners in the Pennsylvania State House. Many Quaker women and children visited these prisoners and brought food, medicine, and drink.

Valley Forge

In 1777, Continental Army soldiers were first issued buttons marked "USA." Hundreds of USA buttons have been archaeologically recovered at Valley Forge.

On December 19, 1777, General Washington and his distressed army marched into Valley Forge, Pennsylvania. The loss of Philadelphia had disrupted supply lines and left the soldiers struggling for shoes, food, and clothes. Washington warned Congress that without supplies, the army would "starve, dissolve, or disperse."

Despite Washington's fears, most of his soldiers remained. There, winter patriots warmed with anger, fired by stories of their lost capital. Their determination grew as news spread of American POWs suffering at Independence Hall.

The hardships of the Valley Forge winter transformed the Continental Army. Valley Forge also tested George Washington, who faced rumors of a conspiracy to replace him. By the end of the winter, Washington had built a more cohesive headquarters staff and knew who to trust in Congress.

At Valley Forge, new supporters came to America's aid. The Marquis de Lafayette had only been in America for a few months by the time the army marched into camp. An idealistic aristocrat, the 21-year-old had proved his loyalty to Washington against his political opponents and his valor in combat as a general at Brandywine. In January 1778, Lafayette wrote that Washington "finds in me a trustworthy friend to whom he can open his heart."

Friedrich Wilhelm Baron von Steuben was another central figure at Valley Forge. A German nobleman with experience in Frederick the Great's army, Baron von Steuben transformed the Continental Army's drills and training. In May, he was promoted to inspector general.

The spring saw an upsurge in camp construction. Soldiers and camp followers were kept constantly at work, building housing for new recruits and digging fortifications to protect the camp. The ongoing work was effective. On April 14, British General Sir William Howe wrote that the American entrenchments made him hesitate to attack Valley Forge.

The encampment at Valley Forge blocked the British from controlling Pennsylvania's interior. On June 18, 1778, British forces abandoned Philadelphia to rejoin the main British Army in New York City, with the Continental Army in close pursuit.

At the Battle of Monmouth on June 28th, Washington's forces nearly defeated the newly appointed British commander in chief, General Sir Henry Clinton. It was the last major battle of the war in the North.

William B. T. Trego painted *The March to Valley Forge* in 1883. The hardened veterans of the army limped into their winter encampment at Valley Forge. Their bare and bandaged feet left trails of blood on the cold ground.

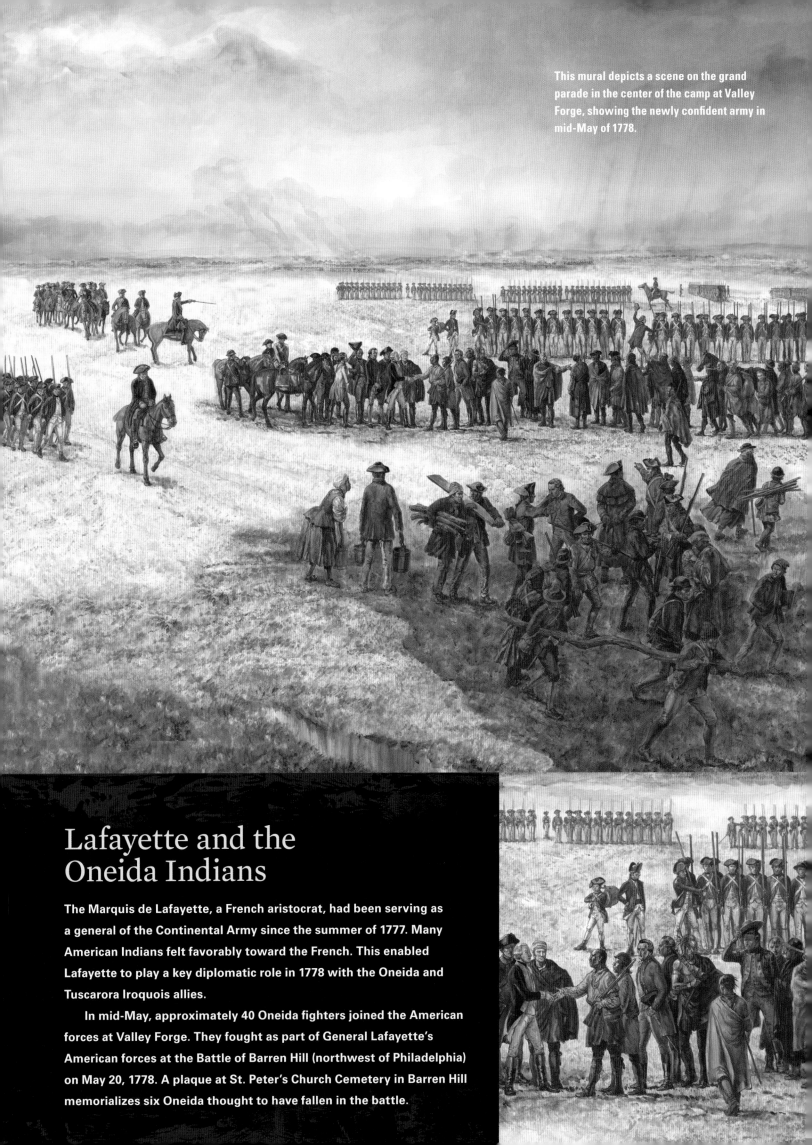

This mural depicts a scene on the grand parade in the center of the camp at Valley Forge, showing the newly confident army in mid-May of 1778.

Lafayette and the Oneida Indians

The Marquis de Lafayette, a French aristocrat, had been serving as a general of the Continental Army since the summer of 1777. Many American Indians felt favorably toward the French. This enabled Lafayette to play a key diplomatic role in 1778 with the Oneida and Tuscarora Iroquois allies.

In mid-May, approximately 40 Oneida fighters joined the American forces at Valley Forge. They fought as part of General Lafayette's American forces at the Battle of Barren Hill (northwest of Philadelphia) on May 20, 1778. A plaque at St. Peter's Church Cemetery in Barren Hill memorializes six Oneida thought to have fallen in the battle.

"The Revolutionary War is a glorious testimony in favor of plebeian virtue. Our military and naval me are sensible of this tru ."

The Museum's re-creation of an armed privateer sloop highlights America's maritime forces during the Revolutionary War. Guests can step aboard to experience life at sea.

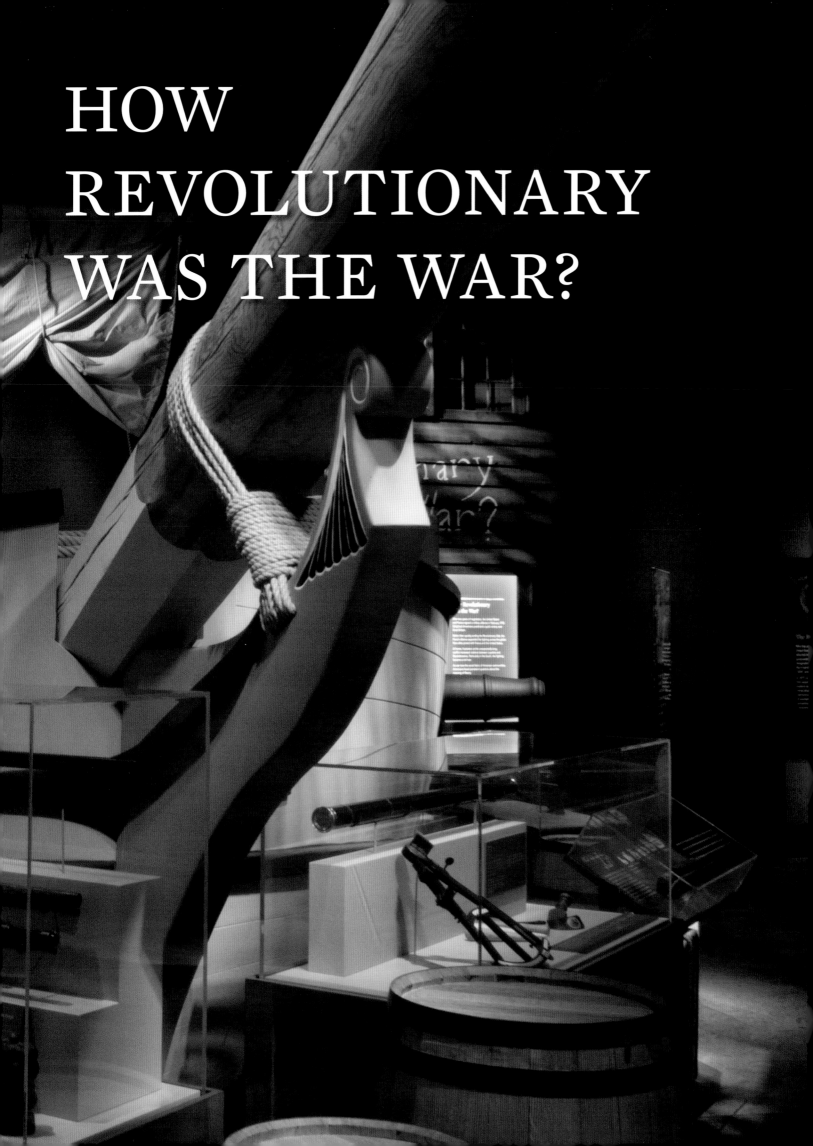

HOW REVOLUTIONARY WAS THE WAR?

The Death of Major Peirson by John Singleton Copley captures the British defense against French forces on the British Island of Jersey in 1781.

Benjamin Franklin

As soon as the Declaration of Independence was signed, American diplomats went to work in France, most notably Benjamin Franklin. Franklin understood King Louis's desire to weaken Britain and the French court's attraction to American ideals. He played both beautifully, spending hours in salons and at French dinner parties to build relationships and having documents, like the new state constitutions, translated into French and printed. Franklin deliberately shaped his image to embody the French notion of the quintessential American—a man of natural simplicity, social equality, religious freedom, and rustic enlightenment.

Through Franklin's tireless efforts, French thinkers came to see America as "the purest democracy which has ever existed." For the French, defending America became defending the Enlightenment.

A Global War

The Continental Congress created a navy in 1775. But with little money and very few ships, it could not hope to match the power of the British Navy. America knew it needed allies.

As an ambassador in Paris, Benjamin Franklin emphasized the ideals the Revolutionaries were fighting for—the republican ideals of the Enlightenment. In October 1777, Continental forces used guns the French secretly sent, winning at Saratoga; months later, the United States signed a military alliance with France. By the end of the war, the combat had forced Great Britain to fight on virtually every ocean and continent around the globe: Spain joined France in its fight against Great Britain. Britain declared war on the Netherlands. And eight European nations formed the League of Armed Neutrality to defend themselves against British naval blockades.

Americans also relied heavily on the old tradition of privateering to counter British naval might. Privateers were privately owned vessels licensed by Congress or the state governments to attack British ships and disrupt trade. They paid their crew and investors by dividing their "prizes"—the cargo and other assets of captured ships—as opposed to paying fixed wages.

Approximately 70,000 men served aboard privateer ships during the American Revolution (about 3,500 served in the Continental Navy). Those who signed on chose their ship and captain. They also had to consider the terms of their enlistment and carefully study the ship's letter of marque. If the ship's paperwork was not in order, a privateer could be hanged as a pirate.

A letter of marque verified that a ship had been granted a legal right to attack the enemy. It also specified what prizes privateers could keep and what portions would go back to the government. During the Revolutionary War, Congress issued nearly 2,000 of these licenses. Individual states issued hundreds of others.

With their global allies and privateering ships, Americans predicted a quick victory over Great Britain. Instead, the Revolutionary War expanded. Frustration at the unexpectedly long conflict increased violence between Loyalists and Revolutionaries. Particularly in the South, the fighting became a civil war.

The Battle of Negapatam was one of five bloody naval battles fought off the coast of India by French and English East Indies squadrons in 1782 and 1783.

BEHIND **THE SCENES**

The Museum's reconstructed privateer ship measures 19 feet wide by 45 feet long. It was built by Independence Seaport Museum's boat-building workshop, Workshop on the Water, and reassembled in the Museum's War at Sea gallery. Made up of more than 1,000 pieces, the replica took nearly a year to create. Visitors to Independence Seaport Museum were able to see the boat under construction before it was transported to the Museum of the American Revolution.

The War Turns South

After fighting Washington's Continental Army to a standstill in the North, British General Sir Henry Clinton saw opportunity in Georgia and the Carolinas. Clinton expected a weaker armed resistance in the South. He believed there were more Loyalists willing to fight for the King in this region—and he knew that British promises of protection for enslaved people who ran away from their rebel masters would weaken the southern economy.

Between December 1778 and May 1780, British forces captured Savannah, Georgia, and Charleston, South Carolina, along with the majority of the Continental Army's southern units. At the Battle of Camden in August 1780, British troops defeated most of the remaining Revolutionary troops in the South. The Revolutionary governments of Georgia and South Carolina collapsed. Some statesmen, including two signers of the Declaration of Independence, took up arms. Other Revolutionary leaders dispersed or even swore allegiance to the British crown.

Initially, Charleston's slaves hoped that the cause of American liberty might lead to their own liberation from enslavement. Some white southern Revolutionaries began to question the practice of slavery, especially after the Declaration of Independence proclaimed "all men are created equal." But the southern Revolutionary states took no meaningful action to abolish slavery during the early years of the war. For many, British General Clinton's Philipsburg Proclamation—which offered protection to those enslaved people who fled their rebel masters—seemed the best hope for liberty. However, Loyalists could still legally hold slaves.

The British Army occupied Charleston from 1780 to 1782. Those who refused to take an oath of allegiance to the crown faced imprisonment. Many Sons of Liberty took the oath. The British offer of protection to runaway slaves of rebels may have led some masters to change sides to protect their claims to humans as property.

South Carolina's 1st and 2nd Regiments wore silver crescent-shaped badges on their caps with mottos such as "Liberty or Death." Meanwhile, enslaved African Americans worked nearby plantations.

British sailor Gabriel Bray sketched this portrait of an African woman from the coast of Africa in 1775.

> *"The Whole Country is in Danger of being laid Waste by the Whigs and Tories who pursue each other with as much relentless Fury as Beasts of Prey."*
> —General Nathanael Greene, 1780

View of Mulberry, House and Street, depicts rows of slave quarters near Charleston, South Carolina. These buildings reflect West African building traditions, one of the many African cultural practices that persisted in America.

Dragoons of the British Legion

The British Legion was a Loyalist corps composed of Americans who sided with the King against Congress. Commanded by British Lieutenant Colonel Banastre Tarleton, the legion included men from throughout the colonies.

Even amidst the horrors of the southern war, Tarleton's corps had a particular reputation for cruelty and mercilessness. Though these stories were sometimes exaggerated, the British Legion came to symbolize the extreme violence of war in the region.

At the Battle of Cowpens on January 17, 1781, 250 of these troops attacked General Daniel Morgan's Revolutionary forces. When Morgan's Americans defeated Tarleton, the Revolutionaries celebrated their triumph over a famous and terrifying enemy.

Lieutenant Colonel Banastre Tarleton—painted by Sir Joshua Reynolds in 1782—was only 26 years old when he commanded British and Loyalist forces at the Battle of Cowpens.

-edom wore
-oat.

Finding Freedom

When the war tore through Virginia in 1781, the state's population included more than 200,000 enslaved people who were suddenly faced with a difficult decision. Fifteen-year-old London Pleasants joined a Loyalist regiment encamped on his master's plantation near Richmond, taking an oath to fight for King George III. Soldiers like London encouraged thousands of slaves to flee to the British Army in search of freedom.

The Battle of Cowpens

After the disasters at Charleston and Camden, Washington sent General Nathanael Greene to command what was left of the Continental Army in the South. Greene immediately divided his tiny force of a few thousand men in two: He sent General Daniel Morgan into the South Carolina backcountry to fight British Lieutenant Colonel Banastre Tarleton. Then Greene moved east to face British General Cornwallis.

By splitting his forces, Greene broke a key rule of warfare. But Greene had a larger strategy. With this action, he distracted Cornwallis and prevented the British Army from supporting its Loyalist allies in the interior.

Daniel Morgan's American troops snared Tarleton's British and Loyalist forces in a pasture called Cowpens near the Broad River in South Carolina. Within the first few minutes of battle, Tarleton and his infamous British Legion thought they had defeated Morgan's troops.

Tarleton's troops had defeated American armies at the Siege of Charleston, at Waxhaws in May 1780, and at the Battle of Camden in August 1780. But Morgan fooled them. He had placed his militia soldiers in front. They fired two aimed shots and then retreated, leaving a solid line of Continental regulars. As Tarleton's men fought these hardened veterans, a column of Continental cavalry appeared from behind a hill, attacking Tarleton's troops from the sides. Tarleton and a few of his troops escaped, but the loss of his legion deprived the British of their fastest-moving and most feared soldiers.

Charles Willson Peale painted this portrait of Daniel Morgan in 1794. Of the Battle of Cowpens, Morgan boasted that he had given Tarleton "a devil of a whipping."

The Battle of Cowpens turned the tide of the war in the South. While British forces still held the coastal cities of Charleston and Savannah, the Revolutionaries gradually reclaimed control of the countryside. At the March 15, 1781, Battle of Guilford Courthouse in North Carolina, Greene successfully used the same maneuvers that Morgan had employed at Cowpens. Having suffered heavy casualties in these battles, Cornwallis abandoned the Carolinas and marched his troops across the North Carolina border into Virginia.

BEHIND **THE SCENES**

The process of creating each of the Museum's lifecasts, or realistic 3-D replicas of human models, took up to 250 hours. First, designers affixed a type of dental plaster to the models' faces and bodies to create a highly detailed impression; then they pulled the molds from the models' bodies, resculpting the figures with plaster, mold, and steel before painting the skin and adding reproduction Revolutionary-era clothing. This model ultimately became the female figure from the Museum's "Finding Freedom" tableau (seen at left).

The War Winds Down

After returning to France, the Comte de Revel was painted in his uniform. The battle seen through the window recalls his service during the Siege of Yorktown.

In 1781, General Washington and French general Comte de Rochambeau met north of New York City. With Rochambeau's force of about 4,000 French troops, the Revolutionary army was now capable of taking the offensive. Washington wanted to strike the British in New York. But General Charles Cornwallis and the British Army advanced into Virginia, occupied Yorktown, and dug in.

Washington and Rochambeau agreed to march south. They moved their forces to Yorktown stealthily, relying on a French fleet in the West Indies to sail for the Chesapeake Bay. They knew that Cornwallis's army would be trapped if several conditions were met: if they could get to Yorktown before British reinforcements arrived, if the French fleet would sail north and cut off Cornwallis's escape route to the sea, and if Cornwallis did not fight his way out before a siege line could be set.

By the time they reached Yorktown, Washington and Rochambeau had gathered some 17,000 troops, including French soldiers, American militia, Continental troops, and Oneida Indians. In Chesapeake Bay, 28 French warships and thousands of sailors stood ready to provide support.

At Yorktown, troops immediately dug a siege line. Then General Washington fired the first cannon. After three weeks of brutal combat, the British surrendered on October 17, 1781. Most Americans believed that Yorktown would soon lead to American victory. But the war in Indian country escalated as Native Americans fought their own battle for independence. For all involved, it was total war, with little distinction between civilians and combatants. Acts of savagery on all sides set a pattern of racial violence that would persist throughout America's westward expansion.

In addition, King George would not concede defeat. He refused to abandon the Loyalists, Native American allies, and enslaved people who were promised freedom.

On September 3, 1783, King George III finally granted the United States independence. For the diverse peoples of America, however, the meaning of independence was far from settled.

Did You Know?

Although Yorktown was the last major battle of the Revolution, the war went on for another two years. Battles continued to be fought throughout the thirteen states, Canada, the Caribbean, Europe, and India.

Lafayette presented the noncommissioned officers in his Light Infantry Battalion with "USA"-marked swords and belt plates. These troops fought through the Yorktown campaign.

> "The troops went to shore without resistance . . . nothing but pillaged houses, ransacked and full of cadavers."
> —FRENCH OFFICER COMTE DE REVEL DU PERRON, WRITING ABOUT THE BATTLE OF YORKTOWN

General William Irvine commanded
Revolutionary forces in the upper
Ohio Valley at the end of the war.

General
William Irvine

General William Irvine, a doctor from Pennsylvania,
led the 6th Pennsylvania Regiment at the outset of the
Revolutionary War. In 1776, he was captured in Canada and held as a
prisoner of war for two years. After his release, Irvine became a brigadier
general. Irvine commanded Revolutionary forces in the upper Ohio Valley at the
end of the war. He encouraged local volunteers to fight, leading to bitter, bloody battles
between Natives and settlers. He was persuaded that "it will be next to impossible to insure
peace with them till the whole of the western tribes are driven over the Mississippi and the Lakes,
entirely beyond the American lines."

WHAT KIND OF NATION DID THE REVOLUTION CREATE?

Abel Buell's 1784 map, *A New and Correct Map of the United States of North America*, was the first American-made image of the whole United States created after the Revolutionary War.

During the war, Cornplanter and other Senecas fought alongside the British and Loyalists throughout New York and Pennsylvania. The 1783 Treaty of Paris did not end Cornplanter's struggle for his people's independence.

Cornplanter

Although the 1783 Treaty of Paris ended the fighting between France, Spain, Great Britain, and the United States, many Native Americans remained at war with the United States. Tensions remained high for decades.

Cornplanter tried to be a peacemaker. At the 1784 Treaty of Fort Stanwix, he and other Iroquois leaders agreed to sign over lands in the Ohio Valley to the United States. Others, however, opposed this attempt to reconcile with the new American republic.

Unfinished Victories

In the mid-1780s, the Revolutionary War was over, but the fruits of victory remained out of reach for many Americans. Families struggled to pay off their debts, and the Continental Congress and the state governments owed huge sums to foreign powers.

In addition, Congress had no power to tax the American people. It had adopted the Articles of Confederation in 1781 as a basic structure of national government, but it could only request contributions of money from the states.

Having won their independence, Americans faced a crucial test: could their new representative governments solve the problems that had just torn the British Empire apart?

Dr. Benjamin Rush was a signer of the Declaration of Independence, surgeon general for the Continental Army, and a social reformer.

This question was challenged in 1786 and 1787, when Daniel Shays, a former Continental Army captain, helped lead a rebellion of western Massachusetts farmers who wanted the same representation in state government as their wealthier coastal constituents. Former Continental Army General Benjamin Lincoln defeated Shays, using his own credit to pay the state militia under his command. He then advocated a stronger central government to make sure that the state could defend itself against such insurgents.

This reproduction mile marker—the original was located on the Boston Road—includes marks from grape shot fired at Shays's rebels from federal forces.

The American Revolution had started with protests against the central power of the British government. Now, as crises like Shays' Rebellion emerged, more Americans debated the need for a stronger central government of their own. In 1787, delegates from the 13 states met in Philadelphia and created a visionary new federal Constitution.

Ratified in 1788, the Constitution established a more powerful national government that has endured for more than two centuries. Yet ever since the adoption of the Constitution, Americans have struggled to balance their ideals of liberty with the practical need for governmental authority. As Dr. Benjamin Rush said, "The American war is over: but this is far from being the case with the American Revolution."

This detail of a crude woodcut portrait of Daniel Shays was published in a Boston almanac in 1787. The uniform symbolized his Continental Army service.

The Constitution

In the summer of 1787, a convention met in Philadelphia to address the crises of popular revolts, public debt, and conflicts between states. The Continental Congress had called the convention to reform the existing Articles of Confederation. It did not expect a plan for a whole new system of government.

During the convention, members hotly debated the best way to represent the people and the states in Congress. Large states wanted more representatives. Small states wanted an equal number of representatives. Ultimately, members adopted the Connecticut Compromise, a system that is still largely in place. It featured a two-chamber legislature with a Senate representing the states equally and a House of Representatives with representation based on population.

The Constitution separated the three functions of government into three branches: Congress (the legislative branch) made the laws; the president (the executive branch) executed the laws; and the Supreme Court and lower courts (the judicial branch) judged legal cases and precedents.

One of the most contentious issues was whether the Constitution would protect slavery. Ultimately, the federal Constitution did more to protect slavery than eliminate it. It prevented Congress from ending the slave trade before 1808. And it allowed slave states, where slavery was legal, to count three-fifths of their enslaved populations toward their representation in Congress.

The federal Constitution was submitted to Congress on September 17, 1787, and then sent to the states for ratification. Impassioned debates occurred between supporters of the Constitution, who called themselves Federalists, and those who opposed the Constitution—the Anti-Federalists. Federalists believed the federal government would successfully represent the whole people of the United States, while Anti-Federalists defended the hard-won independence of the individual states.

During the ratification debate, many Americans insisted on adding a bill of rights to the Constitution. Not wanting to delay ratification, the Federalists promised to add one in the first session of the new Congress. The Bill of Rights was proposed in 1789 and ratified in 1791.

The Constitution became law on June 21, 1788, when New Hampshire adopted it as the ninth state. Ratification by Virginia and New York shortly thereafter secured its power. Rhode Island was the last state to ratify the Constitution in 1790.

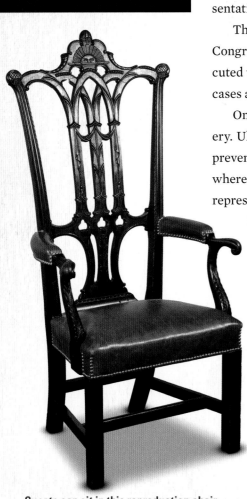

Guests can sit in this reproduction chair George Washington occupied during the 1787 Constitutional Convention.

"I have . . . often in the course of the session . . . looked at that [sun] behind the president without being able to tell whether it was rising or setting: but now at length I have the happiness to know it is a rising sun and not a setting sun."

—Benjamin Franklin, upon seeing the "Rising Sun" chair

Southern states, like Virginia and South Carolina, increasingly depended on the institution of slavery.

James Madison

Virginian James Madison, known as the Father of the Constitution, was one of the strongest advocates of creating a centralized national government. With John Jay and Alexander Hamilton, Madison wrote a series of newspaper essays collectively known as *The Federalist*, which became the most famous products of this debate.

Supporters of the Constitution like James Madison argued that state governments primarily represented local elites. Only the more detached and distant federal government, Madison reasoned, could represent the whole people.

James Peale's 1795 painting *The Artist and His Family* places his wife in a prominent position. Many Americans believed that educated women could play a vital role in preserving the American republic.

The New Republic

Following independence, a new nation began to emerge. George Washington was elected the first president of the United States after a landslide victory and inaugurated on the steps of New York City's Federal Hall on April 30, 1789. Although Washington was widely admired, many still feared that the presidency was too much like a monarchy. Washington eased these concerns by dressing plainly and carefully avoiding behavior that might seem aristocratic.

The change from monarchy to republic affected the nation in other ways. After the Revolutionary War, many Americans worked to secure their republic through education. They believed that only people who had been taught to think critically could rule themselves without a king.

By the 1790s, there was a growing movement for women's education in the United States. English feminist Mary Wollstonecraft, whose *A Vindication of the Rights of Woman* was first published in 1792, argued that women were intellectually equal to men. The idea of "republican motherhood" also emerged. This concept held that educated women should remain at home, teaching children to be good citizens.

Along with increased education at home, there was an emphasis on public schooling in the 1780s. By the 1820s, educational reforms in some states guaranteed publicly funded education. Today's public school system is a direct legacy of the Revolution.

The Revolutionaries fought for equality, but they did not end enslavement. While Northern states passed gradual abolition acts, slavery expanded westward as Congress added new states to the union. In the years following the war, memories of enslaved African Americans who had joined the British encouraged fears of slave uprisings. In response, masters chose cruel punishments for suspected rebels. Ironically, the idea of equality encouraged the growth of scientific racism. When abolitionists argued that "all men are created equal," defenders of slavery replied that African Americans were not fully human.

Despite all this, enslaved people continued to fight for their freedom. In the 1820s, abolitionist David Walker called for a religious and political awakening among his fellow African Americans. The American Civil War ended legalized slavery in the United States in 1865, but the fight for equality has continued.

WALKER'S APPEAL, IN FOUR ARTICLES; TOGETHER WITH A PREAMBLE, TO THE COLOURED CITIZENS OF THE WORLD, BUT IN PARTICULAR, AND VERY EXPRESSLY, TO THOSE OF THE UNITED STATES OF AMERICA, WRITTEN IN BOSTON, STATE OF MASSACHUSETTS, SEPTEMBER 28, 1829.

THIRD AND LAST EDITION, WITH ADDITIONAL NOTES, CORRECTIONS, &c.

Boston: REVISED AND PUBLISHED BY DAVID WALKER. 1830.

David Walker, a free African American, published this antislavery appeal in 1830. He called for a religious and political awakening among African Americans.

After the Revolution, English manufacturers were quick to capitalize on American patriotism. This early-1800s jug shows the great chain of states.

Did You Know?

In 1789, John Adams proposed a new greeting for the president. He suggested the royal-sounding "His High Mightiness, the President of the United States and Protector of their Liberties." James Madison led the House of Representatives in adopting the more democratic "Mr. President" instead.

The Ongoing Revolution

The American Revolution was more than a movement for independence from Britain. The Revolutionaries fought to replace the monarchy and aristocracy with liberty and equality.

Thomas Paine's vision in 1776 was that America would "prepare in time, an asylum for mankind." The fledgling nation, however, was poor. At the end of the Revolutionary War, Congress owed Continental soldiers back pay and bounty lands. Many destitute veterans sold their claims to their unpaid wages and land bounties for only pennies on the dollar. Congress finally passed the first veterans' pension act in 1818. When 18,000 men applied, Congress required veterans to prove that they lived in poverty. Many refused the humiliation of having their homes and meager possessions itemized. Further acts eliminated the poverty clause and extended pensions to men who served for as little as six months. It was not until the 1830s that widows of Revolutionary War veterans were eligible to receive pensions.

As the surviving members of that generation dwindled, Americans wondered if future generations could preserve its democratic principles. In 1858, Abraham Lincoln saw a connection between the ideals of the Revolution and the hopes of millions of immigrants arriving on US shores. Their lives exemplified what Lincoln called "the pure, fresh, free breath of the Revolution."

Yet America's surging growth and wealth relied heavily on the skills, labor, and suffering of enslaved people. Breaking America's poisonous tie to slavery would only be resolved in civil war. Even then, it would take another hundred years for African Americans to secure the legal foundation for full rights of citizenship. Women did not gain the right to vote until 1920. And Native Americans did not receive the rights of US citizenship until 1924.

Since the Revolution inspired Americans "to begin the world over again," as Thomas Paine said, it does not belong exclusively to a moment in history or to any one group. The American Revolution is an idea that lives in everyone—one that beckons people around the world to advance the promise of freedom.

Seneca Indian Thaonawyuthe, also called Chainbreaker, fought alongside the British during the Revolutionary War. As an old man, he still recalled the bloody 1777 Battle of Oriskany.

The iron fence that surrounded King George's statue at Bowling Green park in New York City still stands. Today, the fence is a historical landmark.

"That is the electric cord in that Declaration that links the hearts of patriotic and liberty-loving men together, that will link those patriotic hearts as long as the love of freedom exists in the minds of men throughout the world."
—Abraham Lincoln, 1858

Generations of American revolutionaries have continued the work of realizing the ideals—and the promise—of the Declaration of Independence. (Copyright Picture by Richard L. Copley with permission.)

FACES OF THE REVOLUTION

Many members of the Revolutionary generation lived well into the age of photography. Historians have identified more than 150 images of them, and more are discovered every year.

The Museum's collection of Revolutionary-era items continues to grow through donations and targeted acquisitions.

Collections

The Museum's collection includes objects and documents from the colonial protests, the Revolutionary War, and the years leading to the Constitution, as well as items reflecting the ongoing legacy of the Revolution.

The origins of the collection began more than a century ago when Reverend Burk established the Valley Forge Historical Society "to foster, preserve, and extend the spirit of Valley Forge." He raised funds from around the nation to purchase the original tent that George Washington used as his command center during the Revolutionary War. He also began collecting other Washington items, including his headquarters flag, and other Revolutionary War artifacts. In 2003, the Valley Forge Historical Society transferred its collection to the newly formed American Revolution Center, today known as the Museum of the American Revolution.

The Museum retained several thousand archaeological artifacts from its preconstruction excavation. The staff is able to reassemble those artifacts as necessary.

Since then, the Museum has continued to add to the collection, expanding its collection of objects from the Revolutionary War period of 1760 to 1790. Objects related to George Washington during his years as commander in chief are a highlight of the collection, including his headquarters tent, silver camp cups, and headquarters flag, which marked the presence of the commander in chief during much of the Revolutionary War. Besides the Washington collection, the Museum features items from men, women, and children of many backgrounds, political affiliations, and perspectives.

The Museum of the American Revolution provides appropriate care and preservation for all of its collections, which includes an active conservation program. This preserves not only the objects but also the memory and legacy of the Revolution for generations to come.

The Valley Forge Historical Society's collection was on display at the Washington Memorial Chapel, including Washington's headquarters flag, seen in the case in the background.

BEHIND **THE SCENES**

The collections workroom allows Museum staff members to securely work with valuable objects as they come into the collection. There, staff members also research existing collections and study loaned objects. Although guests are not allowed in the workroom, they can watch through the window as the curators and registrars work with collections items.

Learning at the Museum

Well-trained and highly knowledgeable staff members bring the Museum's immersive exhibits to life with regular performances, demonstrations of early American trades and crafts, and activities—such as Firing a Cannon, Mustering for Battle, and Stories on Deck. Visitors can handle replica objects, participate in one-on-one talks with educators, and imagine wearing the clothing and doing the work of Revolutionaries.

Discovery carts with reproduction objects provide opportunities for guests to get hands-on with history.

Visitors often ask, "What was life like in Philadelphia during the Revolutionary War?" The Museum's discovery center, Revolution Place, brings to life the lively, diverse Old City neighborhood in the 1700s. Located in the John M. Templeton Education Center, this space (along with other programming and learning resources) draws on the Museum's collection and exhibits to present multiple historical perspectives of real people who lived through the American Revolution.

After hours, evening programs at the Museum explore the history and meaning of the American Revolution today with special speaker programs, panel discussions, and a History after Hours series that features talks, demonstrations, performances, and more.

Programs for students and teachers are essential to the Museum's educational mission. The in-gallery experience Through Their Eyes invites young people to explore the major causes and events of the American Revolution through the eyes of the men, women, and children who lived through it. Outside the Museum walls, classroom-based programs provide a more in-depth look into particular themes. The Museum produces teacher professional development workshops, pre- and post-visit materials, and an online Virtual Field Trip.

Using reproduced settings and objects and digital interactives, families learn and play together in Revolution Place, the Museum's discovery center.

Touch a Piece of History

This smooth wood is a fragment of the last surviving Liberty Tree, which stood in Annapolis, Maryland until 1999. It was one of the numerous Liberty Trees that American colonists used as symbols and gathering places in the 1760s and 1770s. Salvaged after the tree was blown down in a hurricane, this piece was donated to the Museum of the American Revolution by the Providence Forum.

———

Please touch this wood from the Annapolis Liberty Tree.

With a mix of immersive environments, multimedia presentations, and interactives, the Museum's galleries foster curiosity and a sense of discovery for guests of all ages.

Opened on April 19, 2017, the Museum of the American Revolution explores the dramatic, surprising story of the American Revolution through its rich collection of Revolutionary-era weapons, personal items, documents, and works of art. Immersive galleries, powerful theater experiences, and interactive digital elements bring to life the diverse array of people that created a new nation against incredible odds. Visitors gain a deeper appreciation for how this nation came to be and feel inspired to consider their role in the ongoing promise of the American Revolution. Located just steps away from Independence Hall, the Museum serves as a portal to the region's many Revolutionary sites, sparking interest, providing context, and encouraging exploration.

This book is dedicated to our founding chairman, Gerry Lenfest, and his wife, Marguerite. The Museum's building, named in their honor, would not exist were it not for their dedicated generosity and Gerry's steadfast leadership.

Special thanks to the following staff for their contributions to the development of this book:

Elena Bras, Elizabeth Grant, ZeeAnn Mason, Philip C. Mead, Kathryn Babbs Miller, Michelle Moskal, Rebecca Phipps, Courtney Risch, Kevin Rossi, Lee Roueche, Matthew Skic, Christine Spencer, R. Scott Stephenson, Megan Storti, Mark A. Turdo, Alyse Van De Putte

Museum of the American Revolution
101 South Third St.
Philadelphia, PA 19106
877.740.1776
amrevmuseum.org

Museum of the American Revolution: Official Guidebook was developed by Beckon Books in cooperation with the Museum of the American Revolution. Beckon develops and publishes custom books for leading cultural attractions, corporations, and non-profit organizations. Beckon Books is an imprint of Southwestern Publishing Group, Inc., 2451 Atrium Way, Nashville, TN 37214. Southwestern Publishing Group is a wholly owned subsidiary of Southwestern/Great American, Inc., Nashville, Tennessee.

Christopher G. Capen, President, Southwestern Publishing Group
Betsy Holt, Publisher, Beckon Books
Vicky Shea, Senior Art Director
Kristin Connelly, Managing Editor
Jennifer Benson, Proofreader
swpublishinggroup.com | 800-358-0560

ISBN: 978-1-935442-74-5
Printed in the United States of America
10 9 8 7 6 5 4 3 2 1

Photo credits are listed left to right, up and down:
Johann Ewald Diary, Volume II, Joseph P. Tustin Papers Special Collections, Harvey A. Andruss Library, Bloomsburg University of Pennsylvania: 55b; © The Trustees of the British Museum: 42d; Alonzo Chappel, *The Battle of Long Island*, 1858, oil on canvas; M1986.29.1; Brooklyn Historical Society: 40a; William Hogarth. *John Wilkes, Esq.*, 1763. Brooklyn Museum, Bequest of Samuel E. Haslett, 22.1178: 18d; Charles Willson Peale. *George Washington*, 1776. Brooklyn Museum, Dick S. Ramsay Fund, 34.1178: 27; Anne S. K. Brown Military Collection, Brown University Library: 42b, 43a, 58; City of Montréal Archives, BM7-2-27_P001: 15a; Courtesy of the Concord Museum, Gift of Mr. Benjamin L. Smith. © Joel Bohy. www.concordmuseum.org: 22a; Connecticut Historical Society: 9a, 22b; *I Am a Man*, 1968, copyrighted photo by Richard L. Copley: 81; Delaware Art Museum, Wilmington, USA, Howard Pyle Collection/Bridgeman Images: 44b; Reproduced with kind permission of the Dixon Ticonderoga Company. All Rights Reserved: 24; Courtesy of Don Troiani Collection: 26a; Special Collections and College Archives, Gettysburg College: 34b; Image courtesy of the Gibbes Museum of Art: 67a; GRANGER: 21; Quaker & Special Collections, Haverford College, Haverford, Pennsylvania: 59a; Brian and Barbara Hendelson: 42a; Courtesy of Independence National Historical Park: 69a; Geography & Map Division, Library of Congress: 72–73; Geography & Map Division, Library of Congress, G3824.P5 1752 .S3: 32b; Prints & Photographs Division, Library of Congress, LC-DIG-ppmsca-19163: 38–39; Prints & Photographs Division, Library of Congress, LC-USZ62-45509: 35b; Prints & Photographs Division, Library of Congress, LC-USZ62-45729: 35a; Prints & Photographs Division, Library of Congress, LC-USZ62-52061: 9b; Prints & Photographs Division, Library of Congress, LC-USZC4-4097: 77b; Prints & Photographs Division, Library of Congress, LC-USZC4-538: 16b; Prints & Photographs Division, Library of Congress, LC-USZCN4-208: 20a; Rare Book & Special Collections Division, Library of Congress, LC-USZC4-5316: 20b; Courtesy of Nick Manganiello: 66a, 70b; Courtesy of the Maryland Historical Society: 57, 77a; Collection of the Massachusetts Historical Society: 32a, 35d; The Metropolitan Museum of Art, New York, Bequest of Charles Allen Munn, 1924: 51b; Collection of the Museum of Early Southern Decorative Arts, Old Salem Museums & Gardens: 10d; Photograph © 2019 Museum of Fine Arts, Boston. *Mrs. James Warren (Mercy Otis)*, about 1763, By: John Singleton Copley, American, 1738-1815, Bequest of Winslow Warren, 31.212: front cover c, 17b; Museum of the American Revolution: front cover b, 2, 4, 5a, 5b, 5c, 6a, 6b, 7, 10a, 10b, 11a, 11c, 12–13, 15a, 15b, 18a, 18b, 18c, 19, 23, 25a, 26b, 26c, 28–29, 31a, 31b, 34c, 36–37, 40b, 41b, 42c, 43b, 45b, 46–47, 48b, 50a, 50b, 51a, 52–53, 54b, 56b, 59b, 60a, 60b, 61a, 61b, 62–63, 65b, 67b, 68b, 69b, 70a, 75b, 76, 80b, 82–83, 84, 85a, 85b, 85c, 86a, 86b, 87, back cover images; National Archives and Records Administration: 9c, 33; © National Gallery, London / Art Resource, NY: 68a; Courtesy National Gallery of Art, Washington: 30b; National Maritime Museum, Greenwich, London: 9d, 65a; National Maritime Museum, Greenwich, London. Purchased with the assistance of the Society for Nautical Research Macpherson Fund: 66b; National Portrait Gallery, Smithsonian Institution: 11b, 75c, 80a; Courtesy of the National Postal Museum, Smithsonian Institution: 16a; Toy Lamb (1760-1830), Gift of the Washington Headquarters Association, Daughters of the American Revolution, New-York Historical Society: 41a; F. Bartoli, *Ki On Twog Ky*, 1796, New-York Historical Society: 74; New York Public Library: 8c, 34a, 56a; Courtesy of the Pennsylvania Academy of the Fine Arts, Philadelphia. Gift of John Frederick Lewis: 78; Philadelphia History Museum at the Atwater Kent, Courtesy of Historical Society of Pennsylvania Collection, Bridgeman Images: 48a, 55a, 71; Private Collection: 44a, 49a; Samuel E. Weir Collection, RiverBrink Art Museum: front cover a, 30a; Royal Collection Trust / © Her Majesty Queen Elizabeth II 2019: 14; © Museums at the Royal College of Surgeons: 54a; Courtesy of the Scottish Rite Masonic Museum & Library, Lexington, Massachusetts, 95.011.1: 8a; Courtesy of the St. Andrew's Society of Philadelphia: 49b; Courtesy of the Star-Spangled Banner Flag House: 45a; © Tate, London 2019: 64a; Courtesy of Mr. and Mrs. Richard Ulbrich: 35c; Documenting the American South, University of North Carolina - Chapel Hill Library: 79a; Vicky Vaughn Shea: front cover d; Wikimedia: 10c; Courtesy, Winterthur Museum, Gift of Mrs. Julia B. Henry, 1959.160: 75a; Courtesy, Winterthur Museum, Bequest of Henry Francis du Pont: 79b; Yale University Art Gallery: 8b, 17a, 25b, 49c, 64b.